Good Habits (and Bad) of the Teenage Years

Loving Your Teens
and Liking Their Behaviors

The 3rd excerpt from
*Teenagers and Parents
12 Steps to Better Relationship*

by

Dr. Roger McIntire

Summit Crossroads Press
Columbia, MD

Copyright 2016 Summit Crossroads Press

This is an excerpt from *Teenagers & Parents: 12 Steps for a Better Relationship* by Dr. Roger McIntire. The complete book may be ordered from Amazon.com, other online bookstores and wherever books are sold.

Teenagers & Parents: 12 Steps for a Better Relationship is approved by Parents' Choice Foundation.

Published by Summit Crossroads Press, Columbia, MD, USA.
Contact: sumcross@aol.com or 410-290-7058.

ISBN: 978-0-9614519-8-1

All rights reserved. No part of the material protected by this copyright notice may be reproduced or utilized in any form or by any means, electronic or mechanical, including photocopying, recording, or by information storage and retrieval systems without written permission from the publisher. Printed in the United States of America.

Dr. Roger McIntire is available for speaking engagements. His books provide excellent discussion material for parenting groups. E-mail: sumcross@aol.com.

Table of Contents

Chapter 1: What Do You Like? (11)

1. Being Loved and Being Liked
2. Being "Likable" is More than Asking Questions
3. Liking and Caring Behaviors are Attractive
4. The Media Can Help Teach Social Skills
5. Sexual Adjustment
6. Create a Dating Policy
7. Set Priorities, Raise Questions and Listen
8. A Disposition Creates Its Own Surroundings
9. Teenagers and Parents Learn Each Other's Habits
10. Amazing Copies!

Chapter 2: Choosing Good Habits (53)

1. Coach Teens to Find Life's Variety
2. Danger: A Human Being With Nothing to Do
3. Practice, Man, Practice
4. Practice Makes Almost Perfect
5. Practice and Reward
6. A Teen's Contribution to Family
7. Fat Cats

8. Matching Funds and Graduated Allowances
9. A Teen's Role in the Family Economy
10. Planning the Token Economy

Chapter: 3: The Not-So-Good Habits (87)
1. Why Do Teenagers Do What They Do?
2. Where Do They Come up with These Impulses?
2. Compulsions and Fidget Behavior
3. Rhythmic Habits
4. Taking All That "Flack:
5. Watch Out for Labels that Mean too Much!
6. Short-Term Benefits and Long-Term Goals
7. Cures and Changes
8. Can Plans for Non-Behaviors Work?

Chapter 4: The Bad Habits: Alcohol, Drugs and Cars (117)
1. Is Alcohol the Most Dangerous Substance?
2. Alcohol and Drugs: Sending the Wrong Messages
3. Drugs and Self-Esteem
4. Medications
5. Drugs and Other Troubles After School

6. Check Changes in Habits and Changes in Symptoms
7. Depression
8. Smoking
9. Cars and the Driving Threat

Preface

All child-rearing theories—about siblings, birth order, genetics, and early experiences—can provide some understanding.

Most of us have a story to confirm one of the theories. Some mention sibling influence: "Roy followed his big brother around even before he could walk! He has copied him ever since." Others support the birth order theory: "She's a third child so you have to expect she will be less aggressive and more artistic." The genetic explanation is also popular: "Knowing her father, it's easy to see where she gets her attitude!" And we all have evidence for the critical-experience-theory: "Ever since he got lost in the mall when he was three, Evan has never been comfortable with strangers."

But past influences cannot be changed. Mom's and Dad's best opportunity to influence their teenager, really their only opportunity, is confined to the here-and-now—the present family interactions.

I often start workshops on the behavior of teenagers and children with this question: "How many here love your kids?" After a moment of surprise, most people raise their hands. Then I say, "Here's a similar question, "How many of you like them?" The pause is longer but most raise their hand again.

Most parents are quick to tell their kids they love them, but liking is more specific. Often, you have to think of something to like.

The first two chapters in this book describe how to develop this most important role in parenting–finding behaviors to like. And then telling your children about what you found. It's your best reinforcement. And it's their best reinforcement, too, once they learn it doesn't have to be said, it just has to be shown.

The third chapter takes up the not-so-good habits such as repetitive tapping at the dinner table or yelling during meals. Parents can usually remember when it wasn't particularly bothersome, but later on, it became a real problem.

At the extreme, such habits can be symptoms of more serious childhood disorders, but even normal adults can develop aggravating habits that drive a parent or spouse to distraction. Kids seem to have a knack for "getting through to their parents."

In addition to providing attention, these repetitive habits can relieve boredom and may also serve a legitimate purpose such as helping a teen-child relax in aggravating situations.

So pencil tapping, foot swinging, and rocking to music may annoy parents but are probably best ignored. Criticism risks giving too much undeserved attention.

Kids have favorite things. We don't mind. A blanket or an old Poo bear for the young ones or even a favorite food may serve as a security post in the swirling waters of life.

The fourth and last chapter is about dangerous habits that threaten the health or even the life of your teenager. When should you cross over and start interfering? How far do you want to go in your influencing of his/her habits? When is it a problem? And whose problem is it? These are the fundamental questions of much of parenting.

The world presents a lot of stress and our kids don't understand much of it. They need their routines, and your suggestions, to manage the turmoil.

Parents have judgment calls to make about these compulsions and need to do occasional soul-searching to discover if the problem is serious or only in the mind of the beholder. How much criticism can Mom risk without risking the loving nature of the family?

Chapter 1: What Do You Like?

First, let's look at your teenager's point of view: *"Mom, how can I get along with the other kids?"* or, *"How can I get the other kids to like me?"*

What heart-breaking questions! Of course there are no quick-fix answers, but a parent can pass along rules of conversation and a little advice about being interested in the other person.

Brian: "So, Greg, how did your soccer game go?"
Greg: "What? Oh, it was OK."
Brian: "Must have been a mess with all that rain."
Greg: "Yeah, you should have seen the mud down at the goal; our goalie looked like a pig!"
Brian: "Our field still had some grass down there."
Greg: "Did you have to play that Kickers team?"
Brian: "Yes. Have you played them yet?"

Brian has a good social habit of an occasional question. Most adults learn early that part of getting along is remembering to express some genuine unselfish interest in other people.

No doubt, Brian didn't keep notes on himself. He just remembers that Greg is interested in soccer as he is and it's just a natural place to start when they meet.

1. Being Loved and Being Liked.

Loving another person and liking other people are very different values. With some discussion, we could probably agree that love is about our basic attitude toward someone, but liking is about individual behaviors.

Many parents tell their kids they love them almost every day, but they say "I like you" much less often. And most teens love their parents but they can be cynical and believe that being "likable" is different. They think it's an "inborn" characteristic and each of us must suffer with our inherited "personality."

But most adults have seen a low responder "brighten up" or "turn around" with a compliment or question that shows interest in his life. How responsive and "attractive" your teen is can change. It depends on his companions and his own effort.

Brian's attractive habit is often imitated and Greg, who is not usually outgoing, picks up the topic and finally has a question of his own about "that Kickers team." Brian partly creates his own pleasant social world. Both Brian and Greg probably like each other because of the reactions they "draw out" of each other.

2. Being "Likable" is More than Asking Questions.

Some kids are likable for reasons way beyond appearance and "personality." We parents know that being "likable" is also made up of specific behaviors; it's a matter of showing some genuine unselfish liking of others—not by using those words, "I like you," but by approving, praising or agreeing with particular remarks or behaviors.

People with this attractive habit are not only likable but also they are often imitated. Therefore, they create more attractive behavior in the people around them. Just asking a few questions, as Brian does, will not turn a person's social life around. He will need to make other efforts as well. And he may still believe that appearance is first on the "Likable Characteristics List" and that saying clever, cool, or funny remarks is second. But he has learned the liking principle. This characteristic is missing from the list, but usually shows up when our teen is asked who he likes. Usually, the answer is that he likes people who accept him, admire him, and want to spend time with him!

Sometimes the view from another person's perspective leads to the discovery that: "To be liked, I should watch out for being too critical and make an effort in my social habits." This can include habits of asking about the other person and showing concern, complimenting, expressing agreement instead of criticism, and paying attention to the listening skillls suggested in, *Teenagers and Parents: 12 Steps for a Better Relationship*. One mom described the difference between her daughters to me this way: "Dianne and her sister Kelly are so different! Kelly can't stop talking and Dianne hardly says a word. It's hard to believe they were raised in the same family!

"Last week, I picked them up from a neighborhood party and when I asked them how it went, Kelly said, 'It was great! They dropped all these balloons on us and everyone screamed! Sally was there, Ann was there, Betty, Millie, and all the boys, Frank, Donald, David and Chris'."

When Mom asked Dianne how it went she just said, "It was OK. Everyone was just acting silly." But Kelly said Dianne just stood around.

Being sociable is like many other activities: If you're good at it, you like it, and you tend to practice more of it. On the other hand, if you don't get started with others easily, you will have a little less practice and the cycle continues.

Kelly's focus is on others; she asks a lot of questions and remembers a lot of details about others that she is forever talking about. Dianne's concern is for her own security. She can't seem to think of anything safe to say.

Both girls have habits that perpetuate their attitudes. Kelly talks a great deal, she is loud, and she has learned about the other kids. Dianne doesn't talk much, she uses a soft voice, and her lack of experience with the others leaves her short on subjects to bring up.

Dianne doesn't have a "problem." She has a quiet

style which sometimes makes her feel left out, but she shouldn't be given the extra burden of being told she has something wrong with her.

Her parents could give her extra social ammunition before she goes into a social situation. Adults help each other with this kind of priming quite often: "Remember (Mom says on the way to her office party with Dad) my boss, Jane, has a boat out on the town lake, and she just got back from Florida. Tom bought a car like ours and Bob Teak's daughter recently made him a grandfather."

These little bits of information will allow Dad to "go more than half way" in starting some conversation with Mom's co-workers—if he wants to.

Dianne needs some help with information too. She may complain that "No one came over to me at the party," but the parental reflex of "Did you go over to any of them?" could be left off while providing whatever information might be helpful to Dianne in thinking up something to start a conversation.

Dad doesn't get a lecture on how to correct some defect in himself on the way to Mom's party, he's just provided with a better chance of doing what he wants to do with information about the others. And Dianne doesn't need more criticism either, just some long-term help as the situations come up so that if she is inclined to join in the talk, the detail of thinking of a topic will be easier.

A person who is good at socializing has many friends; they laugh at the same things and cooperate on the same tasks. They don't seem to try to please each other, they just do. The notion of being pleasing in order to get along with others may seem a little simple-minded and of little use until pleasing, agreeing, disagreeing, fighting and cooperating are seen as special cases of social rewards and mild punishments.

Most teens worry about how attractive or likable they are and certainly some primping before an outing can make a difference. However, like many adults, they think their attractiveness is largely based on their physical appearance while their judgment of others largely depends on what the others do! So it follows that in order to be likable, teens will have to do some liking.

Cool, moody, critical, sarcastic, angry, or bitter people make interesting characters in movies. But in real life, such characters are not well-liked because they rarely show genuine interest in others.

Without making an effort to like others, teens may have uneasy and insecure feelings. At the end of an evening with peers they probably feel they missed something. Liking is a behavior that bears a message to the receiver, a communication that must be sent in order to be received. Consider the following example.

Anne was nervous before John came by for her. When all her adjusting and posturing in front of the mirror was done, the best help would be to plan ways to show she liked John. Physical attractiveness is important, but the other part of being attractive is letting your friend or date know you like him or her. Anne adjusted her hair after the walk to the car and remembered not to slouch when they were riding along. She wondered if he would like her to talk about his football game.

Did Anne look at the date from John's side? If she did, she needed to show it by asking John some questions about his activities, family, job, and school work. She probably needs to do some planning of these topics before the next date. If she did like John, she didn't show it because she was too preoccupied with herself.

Did John think Anne liked him? He didn't know, so he fell into the same mistake Anne was trying to avoid in the first place—worrying about being likable when a little liking would have been a better strategy. He wondered how he could impress Anne: Tell her about the football game? Drive in a daring way? Tell her about his latest success? Instead, he could have sent his own liking messages—asking questions about Anne and complimenting her.

Would Anne go out with him again? Maybe—if she liked him and if she thought she was liked! Will he call again? Anne probably thought that depended on whether he liked her or not, partly true, but it also depended on whether he thought he was liked.

3. Liking and Caring Behaviors are Attractive.

Do your family members use liking behaviors? If so, then preparing for an outing will not be a stressful time for your teen because he/she understands the basics that make a person likable. The moments before a party can be planning time: "At the party I want to spend time with . . . I want to talk to . . . I will show I like (fill in the blank) by . . ."

Natural liking behaviors are consistent attention, questions, encouragement, and praise, instead of preoccupation with your own looks and interests. If you do more asking and listening than you do telling, then you're probably on the right track. Liking behaviors are habits that grow with practice and replace their opposites—silence or criticism, sarcasm, and negative comments.

Answers can be impressive, but questions send the messages. A teen asks about her boyfriend's studying; he asks about her day. The messages show concern—they say, "I'm interested in you."

In marital counseling a common assignment for both members of the couple is to have "caring days"—days when he or she does a particular thing for his or her spouse—without being asked or expecting anything in return. What do you suppose is the request most often listed for the caring day by the wife? She says, "I wish he would ask me about my day sometimes." Out of all the things a husband could say, this simple wish is the most common request: personalized interest and attention.

Liking is not always returned, and two-way relationships will not balance exactly. One person will be required to go more than half-way to make it work. Socially successful and likable people put out more than their share of effort in relationships that are not ideally balanced in regard to effort.

Teens need to live with less than ideal situations at times, and discover when to accept and when to change a relationship, so as not to be unfairly used. Keeping too tight a score on how much you put yourself out for someone may keep things so even that the relationship is not appreciated. A little extra effort with persons at home or school can help smooth troubles as they come up.

When talking with your teen about why certain people are attractive, look at the behaviors of those people. Teens need to discover that Johnny Depp and Angelina Jolie are attractive in their films for a combination of reasons. Their physical characteristics are not easily copied, but look carefully at how Johnny Depp plays in his romantic scenes. He's concerned, involved, and ready to be a part of his leading lady's solution to problems.

Isn't this the fantasy, "If he were here, he would be interested in me, too?" When a film wishes to portray the disillusionment of the common fellow who pursues a beautiful and too-sophisticated woman, the script doesn't turn her ugly—just vain, uninterested and not capable of liking others.

4. The Media Can Help Teaching Social Skills.

Parents can use the popularity of the media with teenagers to trigger listening times. When teens and parents watch a TV show together or read the same magazine article, they can talk it over. Ask teens about the situations or characters' actions. Raise questions and then listen, instead of moralizing. Listening helps teens express their developing views; telling them what to think turns them off to the adult and the topic.

Teens and parents need variety from the daily routine and repetitious discussion topics: friends, school, and hobbies. When Mom and Dad make separate lists of topics they discuss with their teenager, TV programs often show up on the list. Parents may see TV as an intruder to parental influence, but it is also a rich source of neutral, lively subjects for conversation, especially when adults and teens watch together.

> Dad: "What did you think of that show?"
> Lisa: "The babies stole the show! They were cute."
> Dad: "Never cried or needed diaper changes."
> Lisa: "Not very realistic, I guess, but I liked the way the grandpa talked to the twins."
> Dad: "Babies need to hear a lot of talk to learn."

TV situations are not threatening because they happen to someone else and your teen has as much information as his parent since both watched the same show. Help your teens react to and question TV shows, instead of simply letting them be passive viewers. You have your attitudes and answers to life's questions, and TV can help your teens form their views, especially when someone is there to listen and ask questions.

How the media portray sexuality is a good example. TV and magazines sell products by using material about sex to attract and keep their audience. They show sex in favorable ways, while omitting negatives. Casual and irresponsible sex seems like innocent fun with no consequences on TV, but we are not shown the realistic side with stress and need for understanding and intimacy on many levels. We are often spared any discussion of unwanted pregnancy, abortion, and the nine-month stresses of pregnancy without a husband's support—much less the anxiety of expectations and commitment. Television rarely shows the caring for a sick baby or close-ups of venereal disease.

In a short time span the media can't possibly cover the 18+ years it takes to raise a person from baby to adult, or the lifetime commitment of being a parent. Parents who discuss media's omissions with their teens can raise questions about these issues occasionally and provide a means to help teens develop their own adjustment to sexuality.

5. Sexual Adjustment.

If sexual behavior doesn't seem to qualify for your list of priorities about your very young teenager, his or her preoccupation with the topic should earn it a place on the list. The body of a pre-teen may still be undergoing sexual development, but the mind is far ahead.

A parent-coach can help a teen with sexual adjustment by listening as he or she explores experiences, feelings, and issues. Total ignorance of sexual matters is not possible today because of peers and the media. Sex education at school can provide the objective facts, but your teen's anxieties and confusions are not likely to be trotted out for all to hear at school.

Of course, sex is an emotional issue, so a parent needs to examine his/her own feelings before trying to help a teen. Which topics are you ready to deal with? Dating? Differences between sex drives of girls and boys? Sex before marriage? Building a serious relationship? Contraception? Pregnancy? Disease? Decide what you think is important for your teen to understand first; then prepare to be a listener your teenager can count on.

Teens will decide their own sexual adjustments, but parents can influence them. Besides listening, how can you help? You could discuss a dating policy and a policy for going out with a group. The two situations usually overlap these days so you need to set your expectations of your teen in both group and one-on-one situations. What are the acceptable places to go and what places are off-limits? What days of the week are acceptable for dates and what curfews do you have?

It's always a surprise to me how few parents have straightforward answers to these questions, even after serious problems have come up. If they haven't faced up to making a few rules, how was their teen supposed to know what the rules were?

Coach your son or daughter about getting along with another person one-on-one for a whole evening. Explore relationship and sex topics with your teen and keep communication flowing.

One mother told me about a conversation with her daughter that seemed to start with her curiosity about how Mom and her husband decided to have children. But as you will see, the daughter was really looking for information about her own risks. It went like this:

> Marie: "Mom, you and Dad waited a long time to have me and Andy, didn't you?"
>
> Mom: "Well, Marie, it was a long time, but we weren't waiting."

Marie: "You weren't waiting?"

Mom: "We wanted children, we just…didn't."

Marie: "So it took a long time?"

Mom: "Yes, sometimes it does."

Marie: "So you didn't have a baby right off, right?"

Mom: "No, not right off."

Marie: "Lauren said you could have a baby after… just one time—she's always spouting off."

Mom: "It could happen right off."

Marie: "But it wouldn't, if you are careful."

Mom had a choice at this point. She could have said, "Marie, I know what you're thinking and let me tell you you'd better stop thinking about anything like that! You could get pregnant easily, get a disease, and anyway it's wrong to go around thinking about getting into a relationship like that at your age."

Another choice for Mom is to continue this "objective" conversation, talking about risks and their probabilities. Mom kept the conversation away from a confrontation, and Marie eventually asked for her mother's opinion as well as information. That's the best Mom could hope for in this talk. So it went like this:

Mom: "It's hard to be careful in that situation."

Marie: "But if you use the right thing..."

Mom: "What's the right thing?"

Marie: "Well, you know, a condom."

Mom: "Still a chance of getting pregnant."

Marie: "Well, how about something else? The pill."

Mom: "That works pretty well, but it doesn't protect you from diseases."

Marie: "Both then. Why not both?"

Mom: "Both is good. Staying on the pill too long is not good."

Marie: "You could use timing."

Mom: "Not very reliable, that was our problem in having you kids in the first place."

Marie: "This is too complicated."

Mom: "Well, in a long-term relationship you can talk this all out and it's not embarrassing, but in dating, the practical part is too embarrassing to talk about and that's where the trouble starts."

Marie: "I guess."

You may still be worried about Marie. The talk

doesn't end with much assurance about what she's going to do next. But the talk never had a chance of guaranteeing Marie's future; the best Mom could hope for is to provide more guidance to keep Marie on the right path. This is not a place for an efficiency-oriented demand or proclamation and, a talk, too short on facts will only lead Marie to ask someone else.

One mother told me, "I don't have time for all that dancing around. I just tell them." I would advise making time for dancing around—take time away from something less important. Otherwise, you'll never learn what it was they wanted you to tell them.

"Mom, I think I have a problem." We all hope this problem turns out to be simple and not too serious—maybe a tough homework assignment or a fellow student with bad social skills. We hope it is not the forever life-changing announcement. But you might have a moment of fear if you have heard the statistics concerning teenage pregnancies.

How should a parent talk to his or her teen about this sensitive subject? Avoiding the topic and withholding information will not postpone the risks. "If I don't know how to do it safely, I won't do it," is not a popular teenage motto.

A conversation too short, too fast, or with too many family members chiming in is not likely to help. Pick a good time when you can go slowly with time to listen in a one-on-one situation.

Make sure your teen gets the facts straight. One teenage girl told me, "I want to be safe. If I have sex, I always sneak one of Mom's pills the next day."

In the United States, teenage daughters have a 1 in 20 chance of becoming pregnant, and both sons and daughters are at three times that risk for sexually transmitted diseases. This is not just a "girl problem."

Before you talk with your teen, a little self-inspection is in order. What do you want to say to your son about his responsibilities in a relationship? What message does he get in the non-serious moments about his (and his Dad's) attitude toward women and sex? What do you want to say about contraceptives? Abortion? At what age do you want to bring these topics up?

The fathers who cause high school teen pregnancies are usually long out of high school themselves, so caution your teenager daughter about these "older kids" and talk to your 17-and-something son about this temptation.

Alcohol is the most common excuse young women give for making the big mistake. What attitudes should a parent model on this subject?

When it's time to get serious, remember all those listening skills. Keep your pace of conversation slow. Reserve your answers and advice until your teen has a chance to express his/her opinion. Before you give your guidance, learn what they know, or think they know.

Remember that one session on this topic will not be enough, so conclusions with "You should...," "Don't ever...," and "Be careful not to..." don't have to be said in the first conversation. Take your time on this subject, it may be the most important part of your influence on your son's or daughter's future.

6. Create a Dating Policy.

Studies link early one-on-one dating, at ages 13-15, to early sexual experiences. Some parents encourage going out in groups as an alternative to the one-on-one situation. Talk with parents of other teens for suggestions and support.

If your teen belongs to a club or interest group, their activities provide opportunities for outings with the opposite sex, without one-on-one pairings.

Most teenagers and many adults feel the pressure when going it alone for a whole evening of four or five hours of one-on-one dating. Trying to keep the conversation and activity going well can be an uncomfortable experience.

Teens are usually more comfortable in a group situation where the social demands are neither intimate nor continuous. In a group, you are not always responsible for conversation or ideas of what to do. That kind of social sophistication comes later. But in a group, when things get slow with one person, you can always turn to another. On your own in a one-on-one situation and without social competence, it's easy to select a dangerous activity by default.

Coach about dating customs. Since Mom and Dad's courting days, customs have changed, but your teenager still needs your guidance to feel comfortable. We've already stressed attention and questions as listening skills between friends.

Your son needs to realize, as old-fashioned as it sounds, that he is still expected to take the lead to plan a successful evening. You may be able to help with this when you discuss transportation or car use. A son needs to plan something he enjoys and ask his date about her likes.

A teen can help make dates successful by being honest: "You choose the show, and I'll choose the snack place for later, but I don't do horror movies!" or "I guess we could go to that movie, but I give it a 6. What do you think of the comedy at the other cinema instead?" Ways to compromise will be learned.

Both persons are probably thinking "I need to act right!" and they need to see that the best plan is to let their dating partner know about their own feelings, likes and dislikes. Then with some high-priority choices handy, an agreement is likely. When your son or daughter leaves for a date, encourage some planning of what they are going to do. Then build confidence with praise for looks and wishes for a good time. Self-confidence is fragile, so no last-minute criticism, no parting shots.

Did you have someone to listen when your outing was good and you wanted to share the experience? Or when it was a disaster and you wondered why things went wrong? Your teen needs a reliable listener. Chances are when he/she comes home, it will be a bad time for you to bring up your concerns, so other things will have to wait while "teen-listening-time" goes ahead. Weave in some stories of your own best and worst dates to show that the two of you have common ground.

7. Set Priorities, Raise Questions and Listen.

Parents report success from initial talks with teens when they opened communication lines. The important part, and the hardest part, for your teen, is listening. Parents want to make their cases for postponing sex, but your teen can probably only tolerate one point before feeling frustrated at being the listener.

With Daughters. Mom brought up building ideal relationships with Caitlin while they were walking around the lake. Mom had thought about it and had even written down her ideas. She knew she wouldn't be able to say everything, but she had her ideas in mind: building a relationship of knowledge and trust with someone of the opposite sex takes a lot of time, time to learn the other person's interests, values, behaviors, goals, and dreams. Trust and commitment increase slowly from small bits of time spent together. The eventual bond of marriage is built on many times of trust and caring.

> Mom: "What do you want from an ideal relationship with a boy?"
>
> Caitlin: "I don't know, Mom. I guess respect for me and my ideas. Someone who is there for me, someone who likes sports, and has a sense of humor."
>
> Mom: "I think respect is real important too. And trust. I learned to trust your dad when I saw him every day and we talked, over snacks, between classes."
>
> Caitlin: "You and Dad knew each other less than a year before you were married."
>
> Mom: "Yes, but we spent time together every day talking about our pasts, present, and futures. We

> came to know the real persons under our college student shells."
>
> Caitlin: "I'll never find a man like Dad. The guys I know don't begin to have it together."
>
> Mom: "Men take time to grow up."
>
> Caitlin: "They have a long way to go!"

And Caitlin does too. But she has Mom and Dad to listen and share her journey.

Dad should plan his listening session with Caitlin, too. He wants her to understand that when boys have sex, they don't always feel commitment, whereas girls often think having sex means commitment. Also, he wants her to realize that contraception before marriage is more likely to be used incorrectly, but teens don't like to hear that, because it implies they're not smart. So instead of trying to get across his whole agenda, Dad will try to do something much harder, be a neutral, encouraging listener most of the time.

> Dad: "In your family life class, did they discuss differences in the sex drive between girls and guys?"
>
> Caitlin: "Gosh, we heard more about physical differences than drives. But our teacher said boys

have stronger feelings about sex than girls. Do you think that's right?"

Dad: "Well, different anyway. Boys have sex on their minds a lot of the time!"

Caitlin: "Yeah, the boys make so much of it when someone says something even a little bit sexy in class."

Dad: "Guys can be more inconsiderate and selfish than girls about sex. It's good to know that."

If Caitlin continues to find a reliable listener in Dad, he may be able to help her understand her own sexual adjustment and the opposite sex.

With Sons. Parents need to keep the lines open with sons as well as daughters. Boys appreciate dads and moms taking time to listen and ask questions to help their sons' sexual adjustments too.

Before Todd had his first serious date alone, he and Dad spent a weekend camping together. Dad noted the important things he wanted Todd to know:

• If you postpone sex you get to know the other person without the stress, preoccupation and anxiety of sex with no real relationship.

- Waiting means you can both trust each other about sex, and you don't have to hide what you're doing from friends or parents.
- If you wait for sex, you have a better chance avoiding an unwanted pregnancy, abortion, or disease.
- The sex drive is a very strong want, but it's a short-run need; building a relationship of trust and caring is both a short and long-run need.

> Dad: "What does a girl want in going out?"
> Todd: "A good time, I guess, and a lot of talking."
> Dad: "Just to get to know you."
> Todd: "I guess."
> Dad: "You talk a lot on dates?"
> Todd: "Yeah."
> Dad: "Do you ask a lot about her?"
> Todd: "Sometimes. Not much, I guess."
> Dad: "People like someone who asks them about themselves—just as you like it."

Dad's on his way to helping Todd learn about relationships by asking questions and letting Todd explore his problem. Todd may even discover that his need is not as simple as just sex, but includes companionship and intimacy at many levels.

Questions and stories help keep communication flowing.

> Dad: "How was your date?"
> Todd: "OK, but Jennifer and I just don't get along so well anymore."
> Dad: "You're having some rough spots now."
> Todd: "Yeah, she likes those horror movies. We always seem to do her thing."
> Dad: "What did she think of your new shirt?"
> Todd: "OK, I guess. She didn't say. Sounds like she doesn't care, doesn't it?"
> Dad: "A little."

Dad's listening helped and when Todd is ready, he'll find someone who cares more.

> Mom: "How was the movie last night, Susan?"
> Susan: "Pretty good. Coming out we started talking to Jim and his friends."
> Mom: "He's a senior, right?"
> Susan: "Yeah, and he comes on strong. They gave us a ride back and he was all over me! He's nice though. I wish he'd ask me out, but he won't un-

less I, you know, do more."

Mom: "I had a boyfriend like that once."

Susan: "What did you do?"

Mom: "Well, not much. I told him where I stood and we got along, but it was always a running battle. He'd try something and I'd always put him off. It didn't last long."

Susan: "He stopped asking you out?"

Mom: "Yes, we were both tired of the struggle. I dated someone else and 'Come-On-Strong' looked for someone more… willing."

Finding out that Mom went through similar experiences, Susan feels more confident. Let's look at two more cases, Kendra and Derek.

Mom: "How was your date last night?"

Kendra: "Oh, fine, I guess."

Mom: "Just 'fine'?"

Kendra: "Tom and I always end up in the same old argument."

Mom: "Really? About what?"

Kendra: "Well, you know, like about how far to go."

Good Habits (and Bad) of the Teenage Years - 41

Up to this point Mom has been pretty neutral and not argumentative. But conversations with teens can have a turning point if a parent signals her intention to be authoritarian, or sympathetic and helpful. Let's have Mom come up with a question that keeps the conversation in Kendra's control.

> Mom: "What kinds of arguments come up?"
> (Mom interested, not angry or opinionated, yet.)
> Kendra: "Oh, he says it won't make any problems."
> Mom: "No problems? Just like a man! There are lots of problems. For example . . ."

Well, Mom has slipped into a lecture mode, and Kendra is probably moving toward the door, so let's take this one back and replace it with . . .

> Mom: "Well, I guess you think there would be some problems." (Again the control of the conversation goes back to Kendra.)
> Kendra: "Tom thinks there's no problem. Right, for him, maybe!"
> Mom: "Right."
> Kendra: "Yeah, it's no risk for him!"

Mom: "Being pregnant, you mean."

Kendra: "Yes!"

Mom: "Good point."

Kendra's position seems stronger now and straighter in her mind. No need for closing arguments. Let Mom and Kendra walk out in agreement. It's the most we could hope for and extracting a promise would not have as great an influence as Kendra's own conviction that she is right.

Talk of sex with an open channel for your teen to talk, discover, and state opinions will result in a less confused person who is more likely to make reasonable decisions.

Mom's talk with Kendra can expand to the general topic of relationships so that the role of sex for good and bad can be understood. How has it worked out for Kendra's other friends? Let's look at a father-son example.

Derek: "Girls can be such a pain!"

Dad: "How so?"

Derek: "Well, they don't know what they want. They want to go out, but then they get, well, stand-offish."

Dad: "They don't want to go far enough?"

Derek: "Well, yeah. It's not like we're doing, you know, everything!"

Dad: "You don't want to do that?"

Derek: "Well, I mean I don't expect it."

Dad: "Until later."

Derek: "Yeah."

Dad: "You know that you could get in a lot of trouble with sex."

That's too argumentative. Let's give Dad the same chance we gave Mom. Dad seemed to get by the choice between authoritarian and helpful at first, but now he's getting ready to lecture. Dad's last remark starts with "you" and it is not hard to figure what's coming. So in Dad's second try let's give him some "it" rather than "you" statements. That should provide a little less confrontation and a little more learning.

Dad: "It can be a lot of trouble."

Derek: "Well, you have to be careful."

Dad: "You're right. But I was thinking of the social trouble."

Derek: "I don't get it."

Dad: "Well, don't people think of sex as a kind of permanent commitment?"

Derek: "I guess. That was the problem with Tom and Kendra. They broke up in a big argument."

Dad: "I guess that's one of the problems. Sometimes sex makes a relationship much deeper for one person than the other. Especially if they barely know each other."

Derek: "Well, you should be sure of the relationship."

Dad: "It takes time."

Derek: "Yeah."

The "lot of trouble" Dad had in mind in the first reaction can now come up by discussing other people, not Derek. For example, how has it been for Derek's friends, Tom and Kendra? How does the media handle relationships, sex roles, and "trouble"? Exploring the one-sidedness of TV can appeal to a teen's occasional negative focus. You hardly ever get a close look at a diaper change on TV. Realistic decisions will come from realistic views provided by long, open conversations.

8. A Disposition Creates Its Own Surroundings.

When kids imitate bad dispositions, they must use threats in a subtle way because they are less powerful than adults. Fighting back, a teen puts off her parents or teacher and may put off their requests for work. That reaction creates further negative reactions from adults who are viewed by many teenagers as confirmation of their cynical expectations of others.

Consider Lisa at age 14. She has developed a negative attitude and is often cynical and pessimistic at school. You can imagine that it is easy to feel uncomfortable or aggravated around her. At home with her family, Lisa receives a bit more attention, but the aggravation and frustration that others feel usually shows through:

Mom: "How was school today, Lisa?"

Lisa: "OK."

Mom: "Well, tell me about it!"

Lisa: "Do you have to know everything?"

Mom: "I was just interested."

Lisa: "Just leave me alone."

Lisa is a non-rewarder. She is self-centered, thinking little of others and asking little of them. She's no trouble, but somehow she's still troublesome. She brings out the worst in others and then reacts to that by getting worse herself. The cycle continues. To break the cycle, someone will have to be big enough to not play the game. That requires love, because it means performing good social behavior with no support from Lisa, possibly with punishment from her instead.

Lisa herself might grow up enough to be the "someone" who will break the cycle someday. However, in the short run, it's not likely that anyone will spontaneously change. The most likely adjustment Lisa will make is to "give them back what they give me." If they give you bad behavior, let them taste their own medicine! Punishment for punishment; silence for silence, or even, silence for punishment ("They won't get anything out of me!").

Lisa may extend her use of punishment and later, learn to use warnings of punishments to coerce teacher or parent. If demands are not met, she increases the intensity of the demand, and then she uses nastiness or possibly a tantrum. It's coercion.

Adults may learn to avoid all this punishment by

giving in early. Giving in serves as reward to Lisa, but it also rewards the adults because they successfully avoid Lisa's escalating nastiness. It is a common parent-teen relationship where the teen's bad behavior is rewarded by getting undeserved privileges or avoiding work, and a parent's "giving in" is rewarded by successfully avoiding the threat of more bad behavior. It's a case of negative reinforcement for parents and positive reinforcement for Lisa.

In order to have an effect on Lisa, the adults around her will need to model and maintain a more positive disposition than Lisa does.

9. Teenagers and Parents Learn Each Other's Habits.

A teen's most common reaction to everyday problems will probably be to imitate people he or she lives with at home and in school. Children becoming teens imitate styles of adults more often than specific adult behaviors.

Attitudes toward others, conversational style and temperament are the durable characteristics of teachers and parents that are copied. The result is a general disposition made up of habits and styles of encouragement and punishment from others. A teen can easily acquire a disposition almost entirely from the family air!

The disposition to punish and correct others can be learned just as easily as the disposition to encourage others. But to learn to police your disposition is a difficult task. There are no planned consequences for you as an adult, and adults change by practice with encouragements just as children do. So whether or not anything can be done about the dispositions in your home depends on the answer to the question "Can these parents control themselves through conscientious effort and through feedback from their partner?"

The positive approach emphasizes reward—not necessarily material ones, but approval, praise, smiling, etc. The job becomes more pleasant for you as a parent and leaves you with a teen who is still informative, friendly, responsive, and not always wanting to go somewhere else!

A positive reaction is much more efficient because

it says that out of all the things he could have done, this is one of the right ones. A rewarding reaction is more difficult for parents, however, because they must take time to decide what they want to reward and what comment or material thing to use as reward. We're more likely to already know what we want to punish and how we would do it.

If you are a single parent, it may be all the more difficult to say to yourself, as a spouse might: "Don't let me pick on the kids; stop me and point out my good reactions."

The family's disposition can also be influenced by making plans about the small everyday social behaviors of kids. Many parents have developed a poor disposition in their teen by not planning the limits of their demands as carefully as they plan the kids' limits. A teen makes so many mistakes, we want him to do so many things right, and he can do so many things wrong. Without a plan, parents may not be sure what is right and what is wrong or where the limits are, so they are constantly after the kids for this behavior or that one.

10. Amazing Copies!

"Isn't it amazing how mother and daughter are alike!" said Ms. Jones. "That woman reading at the end of the back row just has to be Regina's mother. Regina even reads at lunch time!"

"Yes, it's unbelievable," whispered Ms. Miller. "And I would recognize Bobby Comic's father anywhere. His attempt at a little joke. And Lisa Sour's father sulking while he waits for the meeting to start. You wouldn't believe such details could be inherited!"

Ms. Jones and Ms. Miller are 7th and 8th grade teachers at PTA back-to-school night. They told me that when they were waiting for the first-of-the-year meeting to start, they often played a "Match the Parents Game." It's been their favorite for years and they find their guesses to be very accurate.

Their success with matching parents and students comes, in part, from physical similarities that are inherited, but the way the students act is partly a copy of their parents' styles. It's a hint the teachers find very useful in their game. How talkative, pleasant, sarcastic, or happy each parent and student is, helps the teachers make their matches and they are very successful.

Everyone contributes to the family atmosphere. Each contributor also follows the lead of the others at times—modeling, imitating, and reacting in a manner appropriate to past experience. Respectful, loving parental reactions are copied by their teenagers in their responses back to their parents and to others. The social habits of the kids and their parents recycle through the family, creating the general atmosphere as these habits are repeated.

Chapter 2: Choosing Good Habits

The school skills, social skills, and domestic skills your teen learns need to be put to use right away. The more they know, the more likely they are to take up the activities of a full life, and the self-esteem they experience from being useful will provide some of the protection they'll need when they encounter dangerous temptations.

1. Coach Teens to Find Life's Variety.

Everyone seeks variety in life, but teens seem to require heavy doses just to feel good about themselves and to keep from falling into a funk. "Do they have to do something every night? Why is continual entertainment necessary? Can't teens just sit down and relax for a while?" parents may ask.

The internet, TV and movies give teen's romantic notions of all the adventure and excitement that might be passing them by. They have already developed many adult capabilities and have an amazing amount of energy available. They also have a lot of ideas about the opportunities out there. Instead of satisfaction from everyday events, they seek dramatic happenings to fulfill their need for action.

Adults have discovered the satisfaction of doing everyday activities: job accomplishments, house and yard work, bills and taxes to pay, shopping for a new computer, book, or gadget. These chores are not the adventurous activities a teenager has in mind, but they do provide a need we all have for worthwhile actions.

Your teen's need to "do something" is usually not specific and needs some adult direction. Having several things you want to do helps you get through a slow day or week. Activities don't need to be tennis, skiing, movies, or going out with the gang; they can be puttering, shopping, or fixing things. These alternatives usually don't start out as fun, but they do get rid of the blues. Obsessions with music, video games, or TV may become the substitute for the adventure your teen misses in a world with limited opportunities for him or her. They may also be symptoms of needs for expanded personal responsibilities that provide personal pride.

Fourteen-year-old Maya had a big day coming up: she would turn in the social studies project she had worked on for a week and give a short talk about her science project. The band was meeting, and she would play her trumpet. After school she had to shop for shoes and help make supper. Later, she and Dad were going to change the oil on the car. Nothing very adventurous, but a schedule of activities that helped her feel good.

Thirteen-year-old Brent was thinking about his upcoming day at school: he expected flack for his late reading report, and math was confusing because he had skipped the homework for two nights.

Even when he was not in trouble at school he had a hard time focusing on his work. After school, his friends were practicing football but he was ineligible until he raised his grades.

His hobbies, biking and music, were on hold until he fixed his bike and cell phone. At a peak of energy in his life, Brent needs adult encouragement to do his schoolwork and chores.

2. Danger: A Human Being with Nothing to Do.

All kings, army officers, college presidents, and teachers learn this principle early or suffer the consequences. So again, planning incentives for productive activity is needed because if some structuring is not provided for a teen at loose ends, over the undirected years he or she will come up with some undesirable habits. Teens may entertain themselves in very bothersome ways if they have no responsibilities to fulfill, no opportunities for useful activity, and no reason to expect any benefit from their choices.

The constant watching here is for a teen's opportunities. It's not necessary to see that she always has something to do. Everyone needs a break and has their own pace of living. But ongoing responsibilities provide something to do when the urge hits them—something to be proud of and something that is a source of self-esteem.

A teen needs help beginning adult chores and focus

on important activities such as schoolwork and fulfilling hobbies. Without some direction, you can expect complaining and escape to less worthwhile time fillers, such as TV, lap tops, and mobile devices. Possibly your companionship in the chore would help: do the dishes with me, not for me; work in the yard with me, and shop for groceries with me.

We adults have learned the activities we like, and we enjoy the therapeutic effects. How can Brent's mother pass along these insights? Brent's reaction to her suggestions is not likely to be encouraging, and Mom will have to continue to help with little appreciation from him. Frequent positive feedback for small successes here and now will help Brent try alternatives and practice important skills.

"Brent, if you show me your completed math and science work, you can go to the ice rink with Roger." Mom had experienced so much trouble with Brent and his schoolwork before that now she insists he earn privileges. After her complaints, he always argued, "When I leave middle school I will do a lot better!" Not satisfied with promises in the far-off future, Mom insisted that his incentives come as a result of his efforts now.

Mom checks frequently with Brent's teachers to ensure that his work is up-to-date. Brent responded to the incentives, and they helped him focus on important behaviors and earn a feeling of pride for his efforts.

3. Practice, Man, Practice.

Many jokesters know the old one about the visitor who stopped a native New Yorker and asked how to get to Carnegie Hall. The New Yorker answered, "Practice, man, practice!"

When practice has been lacking, painful experiences are ahead for a teen about to leave the nest. Life has disadvantages awaiting a girl with little experience deciding what to eat, when to eat, what to wear and when to wear it, what to say when making a dental appointment, and how to distinguish between "free" and "on credit"—a distinction lost on many college credit card holders now in trouble.

Without practice in all of these skills in her teenage years she will feel a little inadequate, dependent, and

Good Habits (and Bad) of the Teenage Years - 59

may question her own worth. As she leaves the family's protection, she will need to learn fast in a situation that is not as loving as her family, and she will bring little confidence to the task.

As girls and boys who are unpracticed leave for college or work or both, their parents may blurt out a last-minute barrage of instructions. Practicing to be an adult, requires a lot of parent-planned practice. Whether practice was left out because it seemed to risk too many mistakes, take too much time in the frantic family activities, or was withheld to protect a teen from life's drudgeries, in the end, parents realize there are consequences to reap and now they rush to get in all those cautions: "Be sure you brush your teeth, get your rest, open a checking account, and choose friends wisely!"

The first experience of being away from home can be all the more difficult and lonely if our offspring-now-sprung has little confidence in deciding when to study and when to rest, because parents always settled those questions before.

Many of my college students go to our campus

counselor with the complaint that no one seems to care about them at the big university. A great deal of the "care" the student misses should have been gradually withdrawn years ago to make room for practice and pride in one's self. The only place there is love enough for all that practice is in the family.

One boy came to me to sign out of college. "Sorry you're leaving," I said.

"I just can't handle all the problems."

"What problems?"

"Little things. For example, I can't get my laundry done."

"Why not?"

"Well, I went down to our laundry room and there were all these cycles and settings. Even my underwear came out pink."

"You could throw the laundry away and buy all new stuff," I joked, but then I added, "I was just joking," when I saw his tears of frustration welling up.

"I know, but I couldn't. I don't know my size!"

For 19 years, the little number rode on the back

elastic of his underwear and followed him around with other little notes about washing instructions, but he had no need for them as long as Mom was there. But now she wasn't.

Many of my students managed to survive the passage from home to campus despite painful evenings learning their size and how to use a washing machine. So lack of this practice doesn't always cause a great deal of permanent damage.

But in many cases, a critical period of the teenage years that could have nurtured a feeling of self-worth and comfort with life was missed. Later, complete development of self-confidence may be difficult to secure.

4. Practice Makes Almost Perfect.

All of us can remember the idea of practice in school work and we understand the necessity for practice when teaching something new. But when we are not teaching such things as tying shoelaces, playing the piano, or learning to drive a car, we often forget the importance of practice. It applies just as well to bed-making, washing clothes or dishes, time management and how to get along with others.

If Mom and Dad do these jobs for their son, he gets no practice. It is easy to be overprotective and slow down learning: "I'll take your library book back," "I'll get your running shoes repaired," "I'll call for your dental appointment—you wait." and "I'll be your time manager, you just do what I say." Some parents will protest that if they let their teen do these things, mistakes will happen. he'll be fined for late library books, never get the shoes fixed, say the wrong thing on the phone and waste time until deadlines pass. All true. And each parent will have to make the judgment—is he ready? Not, "Is she ready to be perfect?" But, "Is he ready to gain something from practice?" We shouldn't wait until a teen is ready to do it without a flaw. That may take forever.

Another advantage to early practice is that your student-teen can gain much to be proud of now. It's true you can't rely on a 13-year-old to choose a perfect diet, yet even 35-year-olds don't have perfect diets. But you do need to give over responsibilities so that you can guarantee your opportunities to encourage your teen's progress. A wise parent creates practice, not just for learning, but to improve a teen's self-respect and confidence. As one young teen told me, "I'm not just a kid. I can do a lot around the house."

5. Practice and Reward.

Perhaps you found that, in learning to play a musical instrument, even practice was not enough. And yet practice was enough to perfect your handwriting. What are the differences between your brief piano experience and your "learned forever" handwriting?

When learning to improve your handwriting, you were rewarded not only for the hours of practice but also for the first little successes. You wrote your own name, a friend's name, then a note to a friend and a letter to grandpa. The improvements were useful, shared with others, they had value and practice continued.

But too often the first improvements in playing the scales on the piano produce little or no admiration, they seem of little use, even to the one doing the practice, and scales are a long way from the performance dreamed of. Sometimes piano lessons are successful because learning a favorite piece or popular song was part of the early training. If that consideration was a part of your music lessons, practice probably continued. If not, you may have quit, but I bet you still remember the pieces you liked and the ones that attracted some attention.

If rewards come early for the first little successes, then a person will want to practice more small steps. If only big successes attract encouragement and little improvements are ignored, one can become discouraged along the way, "I'll never be really good." It is not the pot at the end of the rainbow that keeps the practice going, it's the next pat on the back or penny in the bank—and for some tasks, parents need to be frequent and generous with back-pats and pennies.

The most common error when beginning to teach something new is to demand too much for too little. The first steps need big rewards—not necessarily money or tangible goodies, but plenty of encouragement.

"This sounds like bribery," you might say. "Shouldn't they do most of these things without contrived rewards? Can't they do it just for the love of learning? Some kids are good and do what is expected without 'rewards,' don't they?"

To answer these questions we need to realize that those good kids were rewarded—socially and with parental respect and praise. Some start early and well, with plenty of encouragement. They perform so well that they receive a great deal of praise and a snowballing effect begins that is an advantage for years to come. If a teen starts off with good encouragement and is well "rewarded," he keeps going; if he keeps going, he is further rewarded and so on.

Snowballing can work the other way also. Some don't receive rewards or attention for the first steps to good performance and learning. They don't expect praise because little was given in the past. If their parents threaten them, they might do just the minimum out of fear, but even the minimum will disappear when the threat is gone.

So without someone providing positive feedback, a teen misses out on encouragement and slows up or stops practicing altogether. Without practice, more opportunities for encouragement will be missed, and even less practice will result. As he falls further behind his parents' expectations, any performance that should have been encouraged earlier will be ignored because "He should have done that long ago." Now even meager attempts at catching up are discouraged. If his success is viewed as "too late," the "pay" may be nothing. Without some "pay" he will fall further back.

> Stanley: "These math problems are really hard."
>
> Mom: "You're really getting into some hard stuff now."
>
> Stanley: "Yeah, they take too long."
>
> Mom: "You got the first one, you should show your brother."
>
> Stanley: "Hey, Larry, look at this!"
>
> Larry: "We did those last year."
>
> Mom: "And they were hard, but Stanley got the first one."
>
> Stanley: "I'll try one more."

Mom's intention here is to show respect for what Stanley has done so far, and a little encouragement to show it off. Larry doesn't help much, but Mom remains on the positive side and Stanley puts in a little more effort.

Does this mean that all successful parents are secret bribers? No. First, these words are unfair because they imply a situation in which a person is trying to corrupt another person so that he or she will do something wrong and usually illegal. Second, we are not involved in "bribery" just because we expect some return for our effort. No one works for nothing. Volunteers don't work for money, but for the satisfaction that is rooted in the reactions of others. The reward may be as subtle as another person saying we are doing well or as obvious as salaries for Congress and fees for doctors and lawyers.

On one occasion a father rejected my suggestion for encouraging his son's homework by saying, "He should be grown up enough to want to do the right thing without some payoff." When it came out that Dad was on strike for more money and was getting support from a union strike fund, his defense was that he was an adult. With his experience and knowledge he felt he deserved a tangible reward (as well as admiration and respect). His son, without experience or success, was to take his responsibilities for the love of it.

So in addition to practice, we need recognition, respect, encouragement and rewards. With all these right ingredients, success will come and, along with it, the self-respect.

Taylor told funny stories from his school experiences many evenings at dinner. Family laughter and comments made him feel good, and during supper he trusted his family not to raise embarrassing questions about his school performance. Ellen got a lot of recognition during suppertime too, but it took the form of arguments with Dad. Disagreements were a habit because she received little notice for her accomplishments, and she had learned to start arguments and settle for the unpleasant attention.

> Taylor: "So, John was looking the other way as he went around the corner at the end of the hall, and he ran right into Ms. Letty pushing a lab cart with crickets in a box. Boom! The crickets escaped when the cart was bumped and he said, 'Oh! I'm sorry. I didn't mean to dump your crickets. I hope it doesn't bug you!'"

Dad: "What a story! What happened?"

Taylor: "John and Ms. Letty were jumping around chasing the crickets and some other kids helped too, but some were yelling 'Oh! Get them away! Don't touch them!' Everyone started laughing."

Ellen: "I don't think that's so funny. Ms. Letty could have been hurt and so could the crickets."

Dad: "Don't be a grump. It's just one of those harmless accidents that adds humor to the day."

Ellen: "Big joke!"

Dad: "You ought to lighten up!"

Since we understand that payoffs have a big influence on a teenager's behaviors, we can ask, "How can I support the actions I want from my teenager?" and "How can I get rid of behavior I don't want by removing support?"

In Ellen's case, her father could listen and ask neutral questions, instead of challenging Ellen at the supper table. Instead of arguing, he needs to go more than halfway to encourage her appropriate contributions. The effort is essential to change.

When Ellen said, "I don't think it's so funny. Ms.

Letty could have been hurt . . ." she signaled the start of her arguing behavior. Dad could have decided to control his reaction to Ellen's negative behavior. Perhaps his next comment could have focused on the neutral part of Ellen's remark. Dad could have said, "Yes, Ms. Letty could have been hurt and the crickets squished."

> Ellen: "Yes, and John was lucky everyone was so busy catching crickets he didn't get into big trouble. Next time maybe he'll look where he's going."
>
> Taylor: "That's not funny."
>
> Dad: "Not funny, but a good idea for John."

This strategy requires close attention from Dad and that means some planning and singling out of goals. The adult thoughtfulness of Dad and Mom can lead to the cure for poor teen behaviors.

Let's look at another example of specific behaviors and incentives that are related to school achievement.

Dan carried home a great report card. He put it between the pages of his social studies book to keep it clean on the way; it had to be neat when he showed it to Mom.

"How was school today?"

"Pretty good—we got our report cards. Want to see?"

"You bet I want to see!"

Dan brought out the improved card with a smile, and Mom looked over the contents. "Up in math. Up in English. You didn't go down in anything! Really good! I bet our sessions after supper have helped. You try so hard."

Mom's support of good behavior was important. She was as encouraging as she could be of Dan's success, and her compliments must have been a motivation for him. Additional credit probably goes to the encouragement in the sessions after supper.

There were two behaviors in this story: bringing home the report card and doing homework. The behavior that benefited from support was the present behavior. When Dan came in with his card, he was encouraged, he certainly looked forward to it, and everyone enjoyed it. After supper, a homework session will begin, and Mom will continue her positive attention and focus on the other crucial behavior—doing homework. Dan was getting help in both places right where he needed it.

Poor report cards and poor homework make up a pair of behaviors. The temptation in this case is to give punishment for poor report cards, with only a hope that the punishment will "spill over" to more homework effort. Another tactic is to try punishment for both report cards and poor homework. This unhappy solution seems to be a trap for bad things getting worse.

The situation requires an upbeat, positive side. We will need specifics about homework and Mom has a collection of responses that help Dan along with the task.

6. Teen Contributions to the Family.

Parents should gradually expand their teen's responsibility in helping with family decisions, entertainments, and chores. A continuing emphasis on membership in the family confirms your teen's roots and value as a family member.

Sharing decision-making with a teen provides practice with a skill that will be useful for a lifetime. Teens have already gained experience in creating family norms, rules, and consequences. It is rewarding to them to share in planning family purchases, trips, and chores.

How can family members spend time together and yet let everyone do something he/she enjoys? A family meeting in advance of the event can help. It can build excitement about family outings and allow each person to have a say in some aspect of the plans. For example, a trip to a different city might include a side trip selected by each member: visits to a museum, a landmark, a cemetery, a famous store, and a show. A lot of conversation about the choices will add to the anticipation, so instead of a passive, backseat passenger, we might have an excited learner. Afterwards, everyone will still be talking about each other's choices.

Now, after we get back, how can we split up the family work so everyone shares? Input from everyone makes the plan for sharing work a winner. Try assignments, then evaluate and make changes. Enthusiastic cheering and payoffs keep family members motivated. Responsibilities for teens might include shopping, putting away groceries, preparing meals and cleaning up, cleaning house, and caring for the yard and car.

It's an exciting, challenging time when teens reach for adult privileges and responsibilities. Parents improve their teen's chances for happiness and success as adults by gradually allowing them to master self-care and survival skills through contributions to the family.

7. Making Rules Together.

Making rules together means getting household members together to talk over their needs, feelings, and actions and then to turn them into livable agreements.

When poor teen behavior occurs, such as not doing homework, try out one of the alternatives to punishment discussed in Step 4. But if the wanted behavior doesn't come and you give it high priority, then it's time to discuss the situation at a family meeting and make a rule together.

Teenagers and younger children are very capable of understanding and discussing situations important to their lives and families. Everyone in the household old enough to participate should be at the family meeting.

Mom and Dad were upset about a call from Greg's

math teacher. She said Greg had not done homework for a week, so Greg's parents focused on planning for a change in the long term. Dad brought up the problem at lunch.

> Dad: "Greg, your math teacher called to say you need to do your homework. You're getting a deficiency because you haven't done homework for a week."
>
> Greg: "That math homework isn't important. I already know how to figure it. My other assignments are the ones I need to do. I can't spend any more time on busy work!"
>
> Dad: "Greg, we will have to discuss this more, but tonight I want to see your assignment when it's done, before you spend time on other things."

8. Preparing for the Family Meeting.

While Greg did his assignment, Mom and Dad discussed the math homework situation. Before a family meeting, an adults' session is important to air views and feelings and to explore possible solutions to suggest in the event that their teen doesn't come up with realistic proposals.

During the pre-meeting, adults need to emphasize specific actions and realistic levels of behavior and practice communication skills they want everyone to use during the meeting.

Greg's reaction to the call from school gave his parents ideas about ways to support his math work. He needed to be persuaded about the value of math homework.

Both Mom and Dad would share with Greg their belief in the teacher's assignment; she was the expert. They decided that one-half hour of math problems a night was a crucial part of learning to work hard and accurately and applying skills to problem-solving. They would tell Greg that part of earning a living is doing work you don't want to do. Practice at self-discipline enables you to do it. You can imagine what Greg's cynical reaction to such a philosophy will be, but it may still ring true and have an influence. They also examined what they were already doing to encourage Greg's homework behavior, and what needed to be done. They focused on providing more concrete rewards for doing math homework. They discussed different options and decided to give points for every assignment completed. Greg could then use those points toward a movie or other treat. They also decided to share math and logic puzzles and to ask math-related questions, "Greg, what did you learn?" and "Give us a problem to solve."

They would tell of ways they applied what they learned to their life situations, to show the value of his skills. For instance, Mom would tell her story of not wanting to do math homework as a teen, but she finally overcame the math problems one by one. From practice she found quicker ways to do the work and it became easier. Because she finally succeeded in math, she went on to courses using higher calculations, and eventually, a science career.

After Greg showed them an improved report card, they would celebrate his effort with a special meal.

When they discuss all this with Greg later at the family meeting, he might have better suggestions, but at least Mom and Dad now have a positive plan to offer.

9. The Family Meeting.

Young people at a meeting will respect the outcome to the extent they see it taking their needs into account. It takes time to listen to every person so allow an ample period. When family members start repeating what others have said instead of providing new input, you have probably covered the situation.

A regular weekly meeting can be helpful for airing concerns before they reach the problem stage. The rules and consequences the group agrees on may need reworking later, but be encouraged that practice will improve everyone's skills and productivity.

Communication skills need plenty of application at these meetings. Also, parents should not push or expect solutions at every meeting.

When Greg has an opportunity to set policy and abide by it, like most teens and younger children, he is likely to take responsibility seriously. Parents need to make clear the importance of the situation in the short and long run and follow up with a discussion of adjustments at future meetings.

Reasons need to be clearly stated. For example, if

parents don't want Greg's older brother, John, to go out with friends more than one night a weekend for several reasons, they need to say so:

"We don't want to have to worry about your safety more than one night a weekend."

"We think studying one weekend night is important."

"And we want you to spend time with the family doing something special on some weekends."

All family members need to communicate their views of an event or problem, exploring alternative solutions to a situation and suggesting rules and consequences that are reasonable. If parents listen well, the keys to a workable solution can be discovered. Teens have a strong sense of fairness, but if teens do not participate appropriately, parents may need to postpone the agreement or set a temporary solution, to be adapted as needed. An ideal discussion raises issues, explores ways to handle them, and then postpones decisions until everyone has had time to mull over the whole matter. During the interval between sessions, reservations and shortcomings may surface. When a final agreement comes, it will be more realistic because of the added consideration of solutions.

10. Fat Cats.

Cats seem to be one of the best animals at taking human care for granted. Give them food, housing and a warm pillow and they can ignore you for days. Teens sometimes take a similar attitude. During a moment of rebellion, a teen can act on the false idea that she is perfectly capable of making it on her own. Like the cat, she has been misled by a family situation that provides most of the essentials of life free and with no fanfare. You too could make it on very little if room, board, clothing, medical, and educational needs were free! The fat cat problem develops from too few demands for your teen to care for herself or himself and too few requests to contribute to the family. It's time for more realistic responsibility. But when you give more responsibility you will need to add more incentive also.

11. Matching Funds and Graduated Allowances.

Positive feedback for correct behavior is especially

important for teens because they need the message as well as the encouragement. They are not yet sure of the right way to act. Should they try not to be messy or lazy, or is that "uncool?" They lack information as well as motivation.

We all need support and incentives for our actions: pleasant reactions, paychecks, awards, and of course, our own good feelings when we do things we value. Teens are still learning about what good behavior is so they crave a lot of encouragement and payoffs.

A graduated allowance pays off a variable amount depending upon the behavior of your teen. It uses the traditional allowance which is guaranteed and usually unrelated to performance, but guarantees only a minimum.

Responsibilities are listed for the teen and additional amounts can be earned during the week. Each time your teen finishes a task, it is recorded on a chart. Each task has a value and the accumulated amount is paid off at the end of the week.

The possible increase in allowance need not be more expensive for the family budget. As money accumulates, it doesn't all have to be spent on amusements. Consider a matching funds program for clothes, for example, where parents provide most of the funds, but for some items they require their teen to contribute from his or her earnings.

12. A Teen's Role in the Family Economy.

A system of payoffs can compensate teens for contributing to domestic necessities of the family. An exchange system could be set up where an activity receives some kind of compensation. Psychologists call this kind of exchange a token economy because in many early programs tokens were used to represent the payoff. The traditional allowance is one kind of token economy.

Since an allowance system is an inevitable part of family practice, parents and teens alike should benefit from an allowance based on the effort a teen puts toward self and family care each week. You and your teen could agree about chores which need to be done and how much each chore pays off. That agreement prevents a teen from timing requests for allowance according to his parents' moods.

Now you are ready to discuss chores and payoffs

with your teenager. Your teen can record work done on a chart or checklist, using an honor system. This is a chance to show trust.

As the weeks progress, tallies on the weekly allowance chart will become more numerous, and your teen will start saving for shopping. The chart and a payoff time prevent the need for nagging and coercion. When chores are not done by the agreed time, instead of using fines, which undermine confidence in the economy, have your teen make amends, as suggested in Step 4. In this case, "allowance time" should occur with time left in the day for chores to be done if your teen is disappointed in the week's yield.

13. Planning the Token Economy

1. List the chores you think should be done each week by your teen. Consider your teen's starting level, need to grow, available time, and family work.

2. List your teen's weekly/monthly/long-range expenses. Some teens pay for their own school supplies, movies, tapes, and gifts to friends. Others save for big items such as a radio, clothes, a bike, or car.

3. Decide a tentative amount of payoff next to each chore, considering the minimum wage, amount of time your teen takes to do the work, your teen's expenses, and your own generous nature. This is a chance to be encouraging and fair to your teen and your budget.

Points can be used instead of money. When a teen accumulates enough points, they can be cashed in for a special treat, a small party for friends, a favorite meal, or an outing. However, teens need practice spending and saving money to learn those skills.

We hear complaints that the token economy uses bribery and over-emphasizes money. The concern for explicit rules about money and how your teenagers get their share might seem too detailed and too mechanical. But we all need some compensation for our work, and you are paying your teens for work, not bribing them to get things done. The label, bribe, takes away respect and the positive emphasis on earning rewards by honest effort that we all enjoy.

Always emphasize sincere social rewards as well: "Well done! Your work helps our family!" so your teen will value his/her accomplishments in addition to the money gained.

Teens will be given their share of family income by some means or other and, as adults, they will have to earn their own and they might as well learn gradually to earn their own way.

Once the token economy is firmly established, other incentives can be added. The most important of these are promotions based on good performance. This allows for duties on the chart to be changed, improved, and modified as your teen grows up. If your teen performs well on some of the more simple and tedious chores, she/he might be promoted to a better set of duties.

Promotions represent higher expectations and emphasize a parent's respect for improved capabilities. If no promotions occur in the token economy, then the system has failed because your teens are not growing up to new responsibilities.

For example, one mother developed a token-economy program to provide an incentive for her son's chores. After the system was applied for several weeks, the son complained that some of the things he was required to do were "kid stuff." Taking out wastebaskets and garbage bags were particularly unpleasant tasks for him. Mom then added a new procedure providing that if he successfully performed the task for 15 straight days without reminders from his mother, he would be promoted to a new task, washing the car. The chart would be changed, and the job of removing wastebaskets given to his younger brother.

The older son eagerly looked forward to this possible change of events because he liked doing anything with the car; the younger son welcomed an additional task, because he wanted more opportunities to perform duties within the system.

Chapter 3: The Not-so-Good Habits

1. Why do teens behave the way they do?

Unchangeable physical characteristics and early experiences play important roles. People also adjust their behavior to achieve certain payoffs, such as self-satisfaction and enjoyment, attention from others, encouragement, and rewards. Although physical limitations and early experiences are unchangeable, we can change some of the "payoffs" teens receive for their behaviors.

The "why" of behavior is easy to see when we describe specific behaviors and their consequences. Instead of leading us to speculate about inherited traits and early traumas, the "why" question becomes "What happens next, after the behavior?" or "What are the consequences?" Kim is irresponsible or Shanna is self-centered. Then what happens? Someone else irons Kim's wrinkled clothes. Shanna's parents help her even though she seldom returns the favor. Those supports may be reasons for the poor behaviors.

2. Where do the kids come up with these impulses?

Parents are often amazed at the variety of behaviors—both good and bad—their teenager shows. If you find it difficult to sort out what good behaviors you want, then you can see how difficult it will be for them to find out how they should behave. Of all the possibilities, what will they try first in a new situation? Most of the time they will try what worked best for them last time or in a similar situation. If nothing comes to mind, they may try out what you do. If it works for you, maybe it will work for them.

Just as you provide consequences for them, you are also the one they will imitate. Kids may deny it, adults often do, saying we won't do this or that the way our parents did. But then we are surprised to find ourselves acting very much like our parents: "I can't believe I said that, I sound just like my father!"

Your parents found the best adjustment for their problems, so you probably went with their choice, and your teen will follow you. When your teenager agrees, you can support him. That will be a reward, and another habit, good or bad, will have been passed along to another generation of the family tree!

So it's not always genetics, sometimes it's just plain imitation.

Mom: "Carolyn really tries hard to be pleasant when any member of the expanded family comes over to visit. She asked Grandma Mildred if she wanted a refill on her coffee and later Carolyn asked her if she was tired!"

Her husband said, "I think she takes her cue from you; you always try to make sure everyone is comfortable when company comes. It just rubs off."

3. What are Compulsions and Fidget Behaviors?

Carolyn's thoughtfulness may not seem to fit with the usual examples of compulsions such as nail-biting, hair-twirling, and lip-biting but they are similar because they are usually maintained partly by parental attention, the model a parent sets, and by the absence of something else to do. They are behaviors that fill up time and may be occasionally rewarded by parents.

Sometimes the smaller habits may be more annoying. Then we call it fidgeting. It happens in the slow, somewhat boring moments of life and almost everyone does it. At first it can be just the random squirming and wiggling of a teen. We may say, "Stop that fidgeting!" Later on, the little habits develop into hair-twirling, scratching, or ballpoint pen-clicking. Even eating and drinking can develop into fidget (fill-up-the-dull-time) behaviors.

A well-known psychology experiment concerning fidget behavior has been repeated many times. A laboratory white rat is trained to press a lever for a bit of food. He soon learns that the food is only given for a press after a long interval—about two minutes. In the meantime there is little to do but wait. What to do, what to do? A water bottle is available, but the rat has water all the time in his home cage so he is not thirsty. But, faced with nothing to do, he drinks (sound familiar?).

It's not in the rat's nature, nor ours, to do

absolutely nothing. For humans, doing nothing is often embarrassing. So we pretend to read (or something) in waiting rooms, in restaurants, and at bus stops. Many of us wouldn't think of going to a restaurant alone without something to read or at least a cell phone to play with.

So the rat drinks. But he doesn't just sip. He may drink up to two times his body weight in water in a one hour session while waiting for each 2 minutes to pass! Since no rat has a bladder that big, you can see that the experiment requires regular cleaning chores.

All that was needed to stop our furry waterholic was to shorten the waiting time for food—down from 2 minutes to 30 seconds. With the shorter interval the excessive water drinking was gone. The food pellet pay-offs came more often, there was work to be done, and our "compulsive" rat had no time for fooling around!

So now we have two possible explanations for frequent, repeated, annoying behaviors—one, they could be attention-getting and two, they could be fidget behaviors to pass the boring time--they are called adjunctive behaviors. The difference is important.

For attention-getting behaviors, we need a strategy

that reduces the attention for that behavior, but for fidget behaviors we need to also reduce the boredom of dull moments. Take a little extra time for reflection when you first see the beginnings of a "nervous" habit or a "compulsive" behavior.

Rewarding other behavior that is desirable will be a good strategy in either case, but the reaction to the annoying behavior itself should be a careful one. For attention-getting activities you certainly want to reduce attention, but if it's a fidget behavior, there is all the more reason to see that support and opportunity for more acceptable behaviors occur more often.

Sometimes compulsive behaviors like nail-biting happen because the family situation is too stressful for that person. Sometimes assessing the family atmosphere and making necessary changes so everyone feels more comfortable at home is a good step forward.

A teen's fidget behavior is due to down time—the lack of anything to do. At least your teen's view is that there is nothing to do. You wouldn't want to get into a "I'll-bet-you-can't-make-me-happy" game, but clearly some increase in action is called for.

Fidget behaviors can quickly develop into attention-getting or other reward-getting behaviors. Now that boredom has brought on the behavior, what reaction will it attract? "Jumping on" fidgeting behavior can be a dangerous parental habit. If the behavior is not important let's not make it so. Instead let's look to the situation for a way of enriching the moments. Any smoker or heavy drinker will recognize the fidgeting aspect of their habit and tell you that the worst time of temptation is during the low moments—not just the depressing ones, but the empty ones, also.

Your first question about a compulsive behavior then, should be, "Is the behavior a problem serious enough to warrant any strategy at all?" Your second question should be, "Is there anything about the current reactions that could alleviate the tension and add some enrichment to the situation to "squeeze out" moments of temptation for fidgeting behavior?" Along this line, you might consider what activities you want in the situation and what opportunities there are for such activities.

Another strategy used frequently is to reward the

lack of compulsive behavior. For example, one mother told me she promised a dollar to her daughter if she could refrain from nail-biting long enough so that her nails would need cutting. Because this demand seemed a bit too large for a first step, her daughter was also given a quarter for each one of her fingernails that needed trimming because it had been allowed to grow.

Such a direct contingency upon a compulsive behavior must be used carefully. There is always a tendency to do more than state the rule, and nagging ensures that some attention will be connected to mistakes. As with any attention-getting behavior, in the teen's view he or she is not getting enough attention and has now found a behavior that seems to alleviate the deprivation. If you now come along with a new strategy that sees to it that your teen's usual solution (nail-biting for attention) will not work, then you need to look for a newly designated, desirable behavior to trigger your special attention. The new way to appropriate attention should be one your teen can easily accomplish.

4. Rhythmic Habits.

Although rhythmic habits are sometimes symptoms of severe disorders, normal children and adults have rhythmic habits, too. Tapping a pencil, swinging a foot, and rocking to music may annoy parents but are probably too trivial to merit any strategy beyond ignoring it.

When a habit grows and becomes troublesome, most parents can remember it beginning as a less frequent event. This can be a case of parents trying to fix a non-problem and now they have a problem.

A behavior that started as just fidgeting became a gimmick for attention, and then a way to express exasperation at his parents. "Getting through to" his parents now produces a reprimand, a new kind of attention in a situation where positive attention seems unlikely but negative attention is good enough.

An occasional correction or request to stop the annoying habit is not likely to do much harm if his parent's emotional reaction can be kept in check.

> Mom: (Aaron has been banging his foot on the chair leg at dinner for three minutes.) "Aaron, stop

kicking the chair—it's a bother when we're eating."

Aaron: "I can't help it."

Mom: (Still in a very quiet tone.) "Did you finish your science homework?"

Aaron: (Still kicking the chair.) "Yes, it's about DNA."

Mom: "DNA. I'd like to hear about that. Please don't kick."

Aaron: "I told you I can't help it."

Mom is right to provide another direction for Aaron's focus. These other topics will have to become a regular part of Mom's habits before the chair kicking or other problem starts. She will have to be very steady in her conversation. If Mom only comes up with these interests when Aaron acts up, you can see where that will lead.

5. Taking All that "Flak."

One obvious characteristic of a teen's bad behavior is that it generally reduces the demands from his parents. Parents can silence a teen or keep him from acting up by taking a threatening pose that implies punishment. And, of course, a teenager learns and uses the same idea, but since he is a less powerful figure he must use it in a more subtle way.

A teen's threats and lack of compliance make up his version of "flak." Some parents will give in rather than "take all that flak."

Cindy uses flak to put her mother off and to avoid requests for work. But Cindy's behavior is also a result of the fact that the request, in Cindy's view, is just work. There's no payoff for her.

By this time you may be getting tired of the idea that everything has to pay off, but remember that what we mean by "pay off" in many cases is just the honest adult expression of appreciation, admiration, or support for something good or helpful.

Material rewards are frequently not necessary. In your job you probably do many things because you have come to believe that it is the right way to do it or that it will please someone. You don't necessarily do it just for the money.

Why don't you try flak with your boss? Because it won't work, I would bet. And also with a good boss, it never occurred to you to give her any flack because there is consistent support for doing the job—satisfaction and appreciation as well as pay.

Cindy's parents try to bring about some effort from Cindy by coercion and Cindy avoids that effort, if she can, because it is straight coercion without a significant parental reaction.

When Cindy is using flack, she often exposes the situation quite well by saying, "Oh, why should I do that anyway?" The statement is pure flack intended to stop a request from Mom or Dad, but, incidentally, it asks a very good question: "What does Cindy get out of it?"

Although coercing behavior is easy to attempt, planning and providing support is usually better and more permanent. Plan reasonable, positive consequences and opportunities for more social approval to open the way for more willing help next time.

6. Watch Out for Labels That Mean Too Much!

For many years psychologists have searched for solutions to the problems of parenthood. Their searches have usually focused on the reasons children and teens behave—in reacting to parents, siblings, friends, and at school. If the reasons could be known, the solutions could be found. The solutions would make life easier and parenting more enjoyable.

But solutions have been difficult to find because they seem buried in a maze of complicated answers concerning the genes children and teens inherit, the importance of early experiences, and the recent treatment they have encountered from parents and others.

Explanations and theories may vividly describe a possible reason for a teen's behavior and may help you understand the situation. That will be helpful in thinking about the problem in a calm and loving way. However, you will still need practical strategies for action at the moment when the problem come up.

Parents cannot afford the common craziness of doing the same thing over and over but expecting a magical new result. Instead, we could try a new reaction based on the events that produce a certain behavior and the reactions our teen gets for it. That is, what happens next? The search for solutions should always return to a concern for the question, "What happens next?"

Concentrating on behaviors and their consequences allows us to discover how to use our behaviors to change the behavior of the kids. The more recognizable the activity is, the more consistent the reactions to it can be. Therefore a teen's experience and learning will be more consistent. For example, the broad labels we use for teens, "She is messy, he is rowdy," or "He is hyperactive, she is lazy," seem to describe characteristics that are inside the person, beyond our reach. In fact, any mom or dad can influence even these characteristics once they identify the specific behaviors. Instead of shy, a little thought may focus on, "Bill doesn't talk much or look at people when he does." "Rowdy" could mean he speaks in a loud voice and pokes people. "Hyperactive" might become, "Rog interrupts his homework by walking around the room every few minutes." In specific terms, "lazy" breaks down to, "Julie listens to music and naps instead of doing her chores or homework."

The task of being specific about complaints is not difficult. Often both parents and teachers have rules about specific mistakes. The challenging part is in listing specifics on the good side. Most parents know what to reprimand but fumble with praise on only infrequent occasions. Lists of specific teen behaviors will help you plan specific parent reactions—negative when necessary, positive when deserved.

One objective is to influence the specifics and increase the good behavior. A second objective is to send a strong message to your beloved teens that there are many things you like about them. Be on the lookout for sending proper messages. Opportunities shouldn't be skipped.

7. Short-Term Benefits and Long-Term Goals.

While sorting out what happens next, both immediate and delayed reactions need to be considered.

> Mom: "Why does she go running out of the house without a jacket? She knows she gets a cold every time!" (Yes, but that's later!)

Dad: "My friend, George, is just like that at work. He snacks all the time, he's overweight, and he can barely climb a few stairs without panting. Someday he'll be a death-due-to-donuts! Can't he see what he's doing to himself in the long run?" (That's later, also, and George gives in to the "right now.")

Teacher: "I run two miles every morning. Sometimes it's hard to get started on it, but I feel better afterwards." (Somehow this teacher resists the effects of inconvenience right now for a better feeling later. How does she do that?)

Brian: "It's a good TV night, but if I attend every Scout meeting, I'll get a merit patch!" (Here's a hint about how long-term benefits come to work: there's a short-term benefit as well!)

Behaviors tend to follow the short-term benefits at the expense of long-term goals. But with a few positive experiences, long-term benefits can overpower temporary temptations especially if someone supports the effort. How can a parent help this process of considering the long-term benefits of good behaviors and the long-term problems of bad ones?

The one common parental strategy is to try to talk a teen into considering the long-term. Talk by itself is often not enough as most of us dieters know. We need some symbol of the long-range goal right now—a reminder that we are making some progress: a daily chart with marks for successes, a record book, or diary. Teens may need something more concrete such as stickers, buttons, Scout badges or treats. If those little encouragements are given some respect, they can have an effect on the present behavior. Isn't that what compliments from the boss, new titles or privileges at work, promotions, and military medals are all about?

Many ideas for some reactions in the here and now are not contrived tokens, medals, or promotions. They are simply people looking for an opportunity to compliment and praise the small steps of good habits. Being so observant and responsive is not easy, but those who do it have good results.

We all know how our morale is elevated by bosses who are positive and supporting and deflated by ones who only react to mistakes. When work and chores are only for the long-term benefit, a "boss" needs to put in some short-term encouragements that promote the good effort.

8. Cures and Changes.

The idea of a cure implies that some general change has taken place in the individual. Mom and Dad should focus instead on one or two problems, review and correct their reactions for these and then carry them out. For everything else going on, they have to rely on their reflex reactions and the reactions of others. The general cure will have to come from an accumulation of small changes.

When we visit the doctor, we all hope for a quick and effortless cure, a magic bottle with pills that are easy to take. Changes in teen-rearing rarely happen in that quick and easy way. Bold strokes that suddenly "get through to" a teen are seldom accomplished. What your teen comes to expect as a result of consistent experiences will make up the long-lasting behavior patterns. There are no magic bullets. There's only you and your teen and what your teen does, what you do and, later, what the rest of the world does in return.

The changes in behavior brought about by these strategies may be relatively permanent, and that permanence can be somewhat ensured by supporting behaviors that you know are likely to be supported by others. For that, you must observe what consequences follow the individual activities that are important to you. Your effort should focus on single behaviors, blaming conditions inside a teen blames the person and lets us off the hook of finding an appropriate reaction.

Practice implies repetition and, in the context of this book, this means the repetition of consequences as well as the behavior.

9. Can Plans for Non-Behaviors Work?

Be careful when trying to arrange plans and consequences for non-behaviors. Rules that say, "If you don't do such and such (watch too much TV, act too shy, walk on the flowers, sit on your sister) I'll reward you" are difficult—even if the reward is a social reaction. The time of the promised reaction may be too arbitrary. When does not watching too much TV happen?

Better to build your rule around the alternative to TV—something that happens at a particular time and gives you a signal and opportunity to support your son or daughter at a particular moment, "So you're working on your art, it's looking very professional!"

The words we use for good behavior are usually not specific: "be nice" and "act right." Not having an exact idea of what good behaviors should be, we have trouble finding them.

The search is more difficult if "good" is described by what we don't want: "don't make trouble, don't yell at your sister, don't sulk and slam doors just because you're annoyed."

When should you react to "not fighting" or "not sulking?" And when these rules are finally learned, what is a teen to do? What should a parent look for in his or her teen's behavior? Better to think of specifics—help with setting the table, saying something complimentary to her sister, helping his kid brother practice his soccer.

Vague expectations about good behavior and specific descriptions of bad, can lead to a common situation of unbalanced parental reactions with bad behavior attracting most of the attention. This emphasis on the negative can lead parents to think of themselves more as police officers than as moms and dads.

Without specific positives to look for, some parents

send fewer positive messages. Even the vague supports that occasionally surface, "You're a good kid!" and "You're doing all right!," have such unclear targets that they don't influence anything in particular. "Don't talk like that!" "Straighten up!" and "Clean up your mess!" can be frequent and specific, but so frequent that the general message is "you're bad." We need to select specific positive targets to avoid too-frequent criticism.

I asked one dad to give me some specifics about his complaint that his daughter, Kim, was "messy." I thought he could be more helpful by deciding the specific actions he wanted her to perform. After some thought, he said, "I want her to make her bed, put dirty clothes in the laundry hamper, pile her belongings on wall shelves, and dust and vacuum her room."

Instead of accusing her of being "messy," a comment on the whole person of his daughter, he used the list to direct attention toward one of these specific actions. By focusing, he could take one step toward specific changes in the behaviors he felt were important. Also, Dad could begin to plan when he could praise instead of bringing up the old complaints like, "you're messy" that may be interpreted as, "(I don't like you), you're messy."

He chose the best time to talk with Kim about the work, decided on the level to expect from her at first, and was ready with his approval and other rewards for her effort. Then he began to look for ways to encourage improvement in her performance.

My experience with Ryan is a good example of sour messages. Ryan came into our office waiting area and first sat on a convenient chair; Mom chose to sit on the opposite side of the seating area. "Sit over here," she said. He moved to the seat next to her. "Don't swing your foot like that!" Ryan picked up a magazine from the table. "Be careful with that," she said. He turned a page noisily. "Shh, I told you to be careful!"

As it turned out, one of the complaints from both teachers and Mom was that Ryan (!) was bossy and constantly critical of others! Mom had developed low expectations and low tolerance, and it was contagious. In turn, Ryan developed his own habit of being critical of others.

The problem illustrated by Ryan's mother is almost

always the result of a lack of planning. The critical part of planning that is left out is determining which behaviors are important and which are trivial. Had Mom ever thought about whether Ryan should always sit next to her? She said she had not. Why had she told him to do so? She said she was afraid he "might do something wrong over there." She said she had no specific fear he would do anything wrong, she just didn't trust him. Some boys might deserve such distrust, but for Ryan it was just Mom's habit with a little reprimand thrown in. A psychological leash had been put on, and it was jerked regularly.

When Ryan's mom tried the "catch 'em being good" suggestion, she told Ryan how well he was doing on a part of his homework and, another time, how well he had cleaned up his room. His reaction was, "What's the matter with you?"

In the second week, after a few more compliments, Ryan's reaction could melt your heart. "Do you like me?" he asked. Mom said, "Ryan, I love you. Of course, I like you." And Ryan said, "Wow." At 12, Ryan is just finding out his mother likes him.

The psychological leash is worth breaking for additional reasons. Corrections that are intended as reprimands may become rewards over a long time. The leash replaces a teen's responsibility for his own behavior. He just does what he wants while he depends on his parent to make all the corrections. So while striving for perfection, total dependence is achieved.

The corrections with the psychological leash may come to be learned by teens as a nagging strategy they can use on others. All parents know this drill very well. It's the nagging that never dies!

> Rachel: "But Mom, why can't I ride to school with Nathan?" (Rachel is 13.)
> Mom: "I already told you why, Rachel."
> Rachel: "I know, but pleeease! Nathan's a good driver."
> Mom: "No. He just got his license and driving to school is just asking for trouble."

The next day it starts all over again:

> Rachel: "Mom, Nathan wants me to ride with him to the mall, can I go? We're not going near school."

What events maintain Rachel's nagging? It's a topic that brings disagreement and punishment, but she brings it up anyway. The first and most likely reason for this running battle is that Mom and Dad have never held a brief planning session about the problem. Without this planning session, the reasons given to Rachel change from time to time; her parents disagree from time to time; and they lose confidence in these decisions from time to time as details (mall or school) change.

The inconsistency encourages Rachel to keep trying because one day she thinks she might hit the right combination of details and get to go. She probably will.

The planning session would nail down the reasons, pinpoint the agreement between Rachel's parents and give them confidence. It would help by stating the honest reasons for the decisions in detail.

> Mom: "Your father and I have decided you may not ride with boys to school or on errands without an adult. We think other students will get in on it and make trouble whether it's school or anywhere else. When you are 15, it might be all right. Right, David?"

Dad: "Right."

Now will Rachel stop nagging? Probably not, but the amount of nagging will decrease, and Rachel will be a little happier because the situation is now clear, honest, and fair—at least Rachel's parents think so, and it gives them confidence. For Rachel, the structure makes the situation more comfortable than the continual argument, although it's still not what she wants. Rachel's argumentative behavior will mellow because the statement of the rule is concrete and detailed—not much room for loopholes.

Rachel's parents should not be discouraged because there is no dramatic change in the argument. The planning session is to make them feel more in control and less vulnerable to the nagging. Rachel is not going to be satisfied on this topic until she gets what she wants, probably when she's 15 or older. But her parents can be a bit more comfortable knowing they have an agreed-on policy.

As the air clears, Rachel's parents need to stay alert and make a special effort to engage her in more positive conversation. They don't want this vacuum to fill up with other nagging.

Good parental strategies, such as the consistent rules of Rachel's parents and the focus on positive behavior that Ryan's mother needed are habits with important benefits. Parents sometimes develop different habits when dealing with their kids than when dealing with adults. They come to expect something different from their kids and worry about any deviation from their expectations. But often the expectations themselves have never been worked out.

What at first appears to be a high standard of behavior by Ryan's mother turns out to be actually no specific standard at all. So a parent in such a situation punishes (in mild ways) nearly everything and finds no opportunity to reward good behavior.

One teacher I talked to was surprised that Ryan was having problems, "I know he can be difficult, but I have decided to catch him doing well. I focus on finding his good moments and when I find one, I let him know it. I think he knows I'm giving him a chance and that I like him."

Adults expect the same of us, more tolerance,

more chances to make amends for mistakes, and we show them a better disposition. What is expected of us, and what we expect, create the social atmosphere we live in. The adult rule is, "Don't correct or reprimand until a mistake has been made. Certainly withhold punishment, it creates bad feelings." Here's one reason the atmosphere is better in the teachers' coffee room than in the hallway.

Another teacher I know said that as she went down the school hallway, she noticed classes reacting to teachers in ways that were "typical" of each teacher's classes. She was surprised that students could make such quick adjustments as they went from Math to Art to Gym, creating a recognizable atmosphere in each place.

From a selfish point of view, if you were a parent or teacher of these kids, how would you like to spend your day? With teens who are modeling positive behavior, or with teens who are modeling punishment?

The most effective reward we use is praise and encouragement. When praise is consistently used in an obvious way for a particular behavior, results are gratifying. An additional improvement comes when the attitude is imitated. Some parents and teachers may devalue the effect of their positive attention because they only briefly observe an immediate target activity. In the longer view however, a teen's disposition will become a close copy of the surrounding adult attitudes.

The non-behavior rule not only fails the specific time test, it also fails to tell your teen exactly what to do. "Karen watches too much TV" needs to explore what Karen should do. Karen's parents would be at a loss to keep her busy every moment but it's a situation where the extent of TV is the problem. Karen's parents could plan some encouragement for a few alternatives to the chatter from the screen.

Does this mean that Karen's parents should load up on toys, food, and money to lure Karen away from TV? Probably not. Most parents have found these rewards to have temporary effects—except in the case of money which will become a bigger part of Karen's life soon enough without using it frequently here.

For problems such as Karen's we need to look around for something useful that we might encourage her to do. Also, we hope to find something that would have the additional advantage of making Karen feel a little more important. She might be proud of doing some of the drudgery of life. How about setting the table, cooking, sweeping, cleaning, or painting. Painting? "But she won't do it right!" you might say. "She'll mess it up. Cooking? That must be a joke."

Of course it's true that you could do any of these tasks better than a 12-year-old. To get it done right, do it yourself. But the purpose here is not to get the job done right, it's the self-esteem, the learning, and the alternative to TV. How well the job is done is not a top priority.

Chapter 4: The Bad Habits of Alcohol, Drugs, and Cars

When the dangerous subjects come up, what's the best way to handle it? No one can tell you exactly what to say, but first, Mom and Dad might do some intense soul-searching of their own attitudes. Some facts presented here may help with your preparation.

1. Is Alcohol the Most Dangerous Substance?

The most dramatic teen-drug stories in the media involve illegal drugs, but statistics tell us that your teen is more likely to abuse alcohol than any of those other dangerous substances. Drugs often produce the most dramatic problems, but in number of abusers, alcohol still wins. Drug symptoms are listed in the next section, but the first attention goes to alcohol because it's more available and its interaction with other substances can be so lethal.

Alcohol abusers are defined as persons whose drinking habits produce excessive absenteeism from work or school and complaints from friends and family. By this definition one quarter of our teens are classified as alcohol abusers by the time they reach college age. And alcohol-related accidents will still be the biggest killer of our teens until they pass college age. Your teen is picking up messages everyday about alcohol use and abuse.

In earlier generations the risks of alcohol and drugs were most frequently restricted to older teenagers. Yet in these tough times stories of the sad behaviors and sad consequences reach down to eight-year-olds, and the accident and death rates are now peaking earlier in each generation.

2. Don't Send the Wrong Messages.

The way you listen and teach, and the role-model you present, all influence risks in the dangerous business of growing up. The smothering wave of media hype and information will present all the possibilities of the abusive behaviors. Your listening can help straighten out the information; your observations and your model can highlight the successes in following the right direction.

It is hard for parents to keep up their effort because their influence shows itself gradually, usually without a teen's dramatic announcement or abrupt change.

"Dad, do you drink?"

"I have had a beer on a hot day and wine sometimes."

"How does it make you feel?"

"I don't drink enough to feel anything. I've learned it just makes me sleepy right away and sick later. Why do you ask?"

"I was just wondering. John's father was drinking a beer the other day."

"It's not a good habit, and it's been shown to be hard on young brains."

"Can I try it?"

"Maybe when you are older."

I think most of us parents would feel uncomfortable in this conversation. We are in the dangerous area of hypocrisy and not much progress is being made. As far as extracting a guarantee of abstinence from a teen, we may feel impatient with Dad. But in building an attitude, a little progress on the big job may have been accomplished.

The topic is so dangerous that the necessary long talks themselves seem dangerous. When our own shortcomings are dragged out for review, the temptation is to fall back on lecturing. The lecture will be an attempt to extract a promise of abstinence, but the only guarantee of safe behavior is in the long term of establishing values. I would give this Dad high marks for keeping his eye on that goal.

Listening is critical in the discussions of dangerous behaviors. A feeling of confidence and self-esteem, as overworked as those terms are in teen-rearing, are the best protection parents have to offer a teen today.

Don't send the message that alcohol is a problem solver. Your model is one of the best predictors of later drinking habits. Yet families that approve of moderate alcohol use, for example, Jewish families where wine is a part of religious services, do not show a greater risk of teenage alcohol abuse. The important factor seems to be the message concerning the role of alcohol consumption. "I've had a tough day; I need a drink!" is a message that alcohol can solve lots of problems.

Don't send the message that alcohol is necessary for social situations. The message that stress or social inhibitions are eased by alcohol is part of the foundation of alcohol dependence. Using alcohol for its temporary relaxing effect only postpones learning better social skills. The habit also becomes entrenched long before the person becomes addicted in other ways. So, for example, many people not yet addicted can't enjoy a party until alcohol has had its effect.

TV and other media glamorize alcohol and imply that alcohol is essential to having a good time. "Things go better with Bud" is not necessarily true, as many of us adults have learned.

Don't send the message that behavior under the influence of alcohol is somehow more sincere, natural or free. Teens often think less thoughtful behavior is somehow more genuine. The notion that because behavior under the influence is less filtered by inhibitions and thoughtfulness shouldn't lead to the conclusion that the actions are better. Inhibitions have been learned from experience, and thoughtfulness is a precious human quality.

Parents need to set a healthy model of problem-solving based on skills and strategies. When teens depend on alcohol to break down social inhibitions, the breakdown of sexual inhibitions will quickly become the next bad habit. Intoxication is the most common reason given for unsafe sex in surveys of teenagers.

Spending time with your teen sends the message that your teen is a valuable person. A teen who feels valued and capable is less likely to start using alcohol than teens who feel they have "nothing to lose." Recognize your teen as an increasingly capable, valued family member.

3. Drugs and Self-esteem.

I'm not going to have a drink for lunch today, nor drugs this afternoon. The statistics would say you will probably avoid the same things. Why? Because we both feel we have too much to lose! We have family and work responsibilities and goals we have set for ourselves. We hope to make a contribution to our community and family and have some success in our jobs. Too much to lose—that's how we see ourselves.

Who will point out what wonderful talents and potentials a teen has to lose? My conversation with a drug-experimenting pre-teen is tragically typical:

> "So let me get this all straight. You took some white powder your friend had in his garage, put it on a piece of glass in a little row. Then you took a straw and sucked it up your nose?"
>
> "Well, yeah."
>
> "What about the dirt, let alone the stuff itself. How could you be sure it was clean or even made of what your friend said it was?"
>
> "Well, I didn't know, but I figure, you know, what have I got to lose?"
>
> (My parent outrage almost pops out.) "What have you got to lose!? You've got your whole life ahead of you..."

I know what I have to lose, why doesn't this kid

know what he has to lose? All those lectures in school—about health, brain damage, infection, addiction, and the violence of the people involved in these trades—and he still can ask, "What do I have to lose?" The lectures are to groups, of course, and they leave out the personal abilities, individual prospects and talents of the individuals. Who will tell our sons and daughters what they, personally, have to lose?

How does a teen learn to value himself, learn what he has to lose? That self-respect will come from developing competencies—even everyday ones like cooking, keeping track of money, and doing domestic chores. One of the best protections against dangerous behaviors is the parental habit of providing satisfying tasks that build confidence.

One 12-year-old boy said to me that he told his friends he couldn't cruise the mall that day because, "I make dinner on Tuesdays and I already bought the stuff." There's a small step in the direction of self-confidence.

4. Medications: "I didn't get my pill today, can I help it?"

What's the answer to those annoying outbursts from the kids—the crying fits and the hyperactivity? Even when medications are necessary both parents and physicians are worried about long-term effects and hope to add natural long-term remedies that will provide a more fundamental adjustment.

Parents may view the problem as a product of unfortunate circumstances. For example, a parent will say, "He has a hard time behaving because he was upset when his father and I divorced." Or, "He was upset when I remarried." Other parents suspect that bipolar symptoms exist in one or both sides of the family tree. Others complain their child-teen rejects discipline because his or her father won't cooperate with his wife or both parents agree with his teacher who said, "He might have ADHD (attention deficit and hyperactivity disorder)."

Of course any of these speculations could be true, or partly true, but regardless of underlying causes, changing a child-teen's behavior using careful parental reactions may hold the only hope for long-term improvement.

Studies by the U.S. Department of Agriculture show children and teens guzzle 64 gallons of soft drinks a year with an average of 38 milligrams of caffeine in every ounce. For adults, it's coffee and, if it's fancy coffee, the caffeine may be as high as 200 milligrams per cup.

After the temporary boost in energy, there's the inevitable drop in energy and disposition that follows. A re-supply of caffeine will produce another burst of energy, but an addiction is beginning to form just to avoid the downturn-aftereffect. Addiction is fundamentally a negative reinforcement effect

Hofstra University Professor Jennifer Schare studied 400 preschoolers for a year and found that the heavy users of caffeine had more "uncontrollable energy," which could be, and occasionally was, diagnosed as ADHD. If caffeine is occasional, provided at school but not at home, for example, a "bipolar disorder" might be suspected. At school he is wired and always in trouble, but at home he calms down, but is grumpy.

Caffeine effects and the additional sleep disturbance that comes with them, provide pharmaceutical companies with a host of prescriptions for "disturbed" children.

Physicians often recommend less than 100 milligrams of caffeine per day—two ounces of most colas—for the whole day. Why they recommend any at all is hard to understand.

In addition to a diet that contains caffeine and sugar in large quantities, food allergies can add to the problem. In the United States, processed foods contain nearly 7,000 new additives all approved for use in our food, and most were not heard of a century ago. By contrast, Northern Europeans have approved only about 70 of the 7,000 food additives that are legal over here. That may explain some of our expanding allergies.

The National Institutes of Health reports that 50 million Americans suffer from allergic diseases and 54 percent test positive for one or more allergens. The most common disruptive culprits in children's diet besides caffeine and sugar are milk products, citrus fruits, nuts, tomatoes, bananas and certain food additives.

"Food intolerances" occur when the digestive

process rejects a certain kind of food. Other problems are food allergies in which certain (usually stomach) tissues are irritated by the food. In either case, keeping careful records of what your teenager eats and when he acts up can identify foods that produce behavioral side effects.

A teenager who is sensitive to particular foods is likely to be more frequently irritated by parents, teachers and siblings. He or she is not likely to understand that disrupted sleep and the resulting unhappiness may be an additional allergy symptom along with his/her runny nose, stuffiness, wheezing, stomach ache, itchy eyes or muscle ache. Even his or her parents may not recognize the connection.

Parents should be cautious in focusing on one solution for a troublesome child. Here's a true example.

When Jeff was six, he was a model child. He was easy-going and seldom any trouble at school, but when he started second grade, he became agitated and impatient and fought with other students. Tantrums became a daily burden at home and in school. At home the tantrums usually built up around bedtime or later at night when he woke up restless and irritated.

Had he been assigned to a bad teacher? Did something happen at home?

I knew Jeff's mother well. She was a steady, dedicated and loving mom. Because of the surprising change in Jeff's character, I asked her to keep a record of everything Jeff ate and when disruptions happened. Although Jeff was already on some medication for his disruptive behavior, Mom took it as a challenge to note every scrap and snack that he had. In six weeks her records showed a peculiar but common event: Every time Jeff had pizza, his behavior got worse.

So we started the pizza experiment. No pizza for two weeks and the frequency of his tantrums went down a little, but his troubles at school and home continued.

There was no dramatic result until Jeff's mom (remember, she's the dedicated type) declared all tomato products off limits for the family. That's not an easy task when you think about all the sources – ketchup, salads, pizzas, salad dressings, spaghetti sauce, casseroles and the list goes on. But it turned out Jeff had an allergy.

Without tomatoes, Jeff's old self started coming back, but every time he slipped up (one time we discovered tomato was in the salad dressing), the irritations returned. To protect Jeff (and everyone else), the whole family stayed off tomatoes.

Where do such allergies come from? It's a mystery how we get these sensitivities, but our expanding diet in the U.S. certainly helps us find them. Oranges from Florida are not just a holiday treat any more, and milk no longer comes from a farm in your county. You can't even be sure your food comes from this hemisphere. The greater the variety of food sources you sample, the more likely you are to take in something that disagrees with you.

Jeff, by the way, grew up to be an emergency room physician. He is still his easy-going self, and he's still off tomatoes.

Certainly diet, allergies and parental habits play a role in these problems. Even if medications are already a part of the answer, a record of bad behavior as well as allergic reactions, variations in parental habits and diet may show other sources of the problem.

Nevertheless, 350 million doses of Ritalin, Adderall, and Dexedrine will be given this year in the United States to control bad behavior in children—triple the doses given in all other countries put together. In many cases these medications are helpful, but allergy testing and careful recording of everything a child-teen eats and the time he eats it can show aggravating sensitivities that cause family problems.

Even a teenager diagnosed with Autism or ADHD is not merely afflicted with one wrong process. Diet and what happens next still influence bad habits. The thoughtful use of reactions and consequences, watching for good behaviors to highlight and encouraging self-esteem through useful tasks, all of these remain a part of the answer to bad social habits.

Seasonal Affective Syndrome turned out to be eight-year-old Carl's problem discovered when his Mom kept records over the weeks of a fall semester. As the days grew shorter, Carl's temper grew shorter. When a set of bright fluorescent lights were added to his dark morning hours, Carl's behavior improved.

Carl also had problems with psychoactive

substances—sugar and caffeine. Removing these sources will nearly always be part of the answer.

Prescriptions can be a convenient answer to common rowdiness, sleeplessness and school problems, but medications can cover up other causes.

Start with a record of the most likely culprits: caffeine, sugar, chocolate, eggs, and milk products. Draw up a chart with the days marked down the side and hours across the top. Tape it on the refrigerator.

Try to record the time and date of every bit of these foods that your adolescent eats. Very small amounts can trigger reactions. Many adults complain of sleep problems or headaches after one cup of tea, even in the early morning, while others have problems only if they drink tea or coffee before bed.

Also, record any other factors that might be relevant. The kids will not see these connections in themselves. One teen who had violent tantrums over the slightest problem turned out to be allergic to chocolate. Even a small brownie after school extracted a price in the family evening. The source wasn't discovered until Mom brought in three weeks of recordings of his snacks, meals and tantrums.

Another Mom complained that after her always-pleasant son turned four, "he became mean and angry and yelled a lot." She agreed to record her rating of his behavior every hour they were together – 1 for very nice, 2 for just a slight problem, 5 for getting mad about something trivial, 10 for a full, losing-it tantrum—usually more than one a day. She also recorded everything he ate at all snacks and meals. Eggs turned out to be a big part of the problem. No hives, no itchy eyes or stomach aches, just irritation and prickliness.

Since behaviors are partly controlled by what happens before and after, I also ask parents to include a record of the events just before and after the problem behavior surfaces. Two hours of TV right before the melt-down or an entertaining argument with Mom can indicate an answer that would help as much as any pill.

The solution will also have to include what is good about our problem-teenager's behavior. What do we want to encourage and how can we encourage it? If he does his homework, then what happens? Do we look it over and admire the work or go on to getting dinner ready because, for the moment, the problem is solved?

Medications can be life savers for parents suffering with a severely disturbed child. Drug companies have a right to be proud of the help they provide. But it is not right to belittle environmental effects just because medications can reduce the symptoms.

Every parent has been amazed by a healthy teen finding 200 ways to sit on a chair, 10 ways to lose his hat, and 30 ways to tangle shoelaces. Activity, even hyperactivity, seems to be just part of growing up.

But one child in ten suffers from behavioral disorders such as attention deficit/hyperactivity disorder (ADHD), separation anxiety, or social phobia. And about 3.4 million U.S. children under 18 are said to be seriously depressed. Ritalin and similar medications are life-savers and family-savers for those situations in which a child or teenager is extremely agitated for long periods every day.

5. Drugs and Other Troubles After School.

The prime time for juvenile crime is from 2 to 6 p.m. You might think it would be at night, but for this young age group, a survey found violent juvenile crime peaked between 3 and 4 p.m. "Fight Crime: Invest in Kids of California," a nonprofit organization, conducted the survey of their state's law enforcement agencies in 1999.

Even in the rest of the nation, after-school hours are the most dangerous hours for serious car accidents involving teenagers as well as juvenile crime. Vandalism, theft and violent crimes are reduced when kids attend after-school programs. Without continued support from parents and schools for a variety of after-school programs, troubles multiply.

Some parent groups meet regularly to talk over their teens' situation at school and plans for sharing of after-school supervision. Parent groups can have healthy effects and relieve the loneliness a parent can feel if things start to go wrong. Parents also gain strength from these talks and from agreements to enforce standards for TV, for computer time and sell phone time.

After-school programs are not the whole answer to the drug problem, but an understanding of the many circumstances that sometimes influence drug taking can help.

We were all shocked in the 60's and 70's to find drugs becoming common in affluent schools. We should have known that these would be the most obvious targets. Addicts need money, lots of money, and they hope to get it from your kids. A pusher isn't interested in a kid who doesn't have much money. Your teen should not carry any more money than necessary to school or afternoon outings.

Parents should also stay informed about the money their teens have. How much does she make from her job? Where does her money go? Better spent on clothes and fun than available for trouble. Just some conversations about weekly activities ought to keep parents up to date without prying. If things don't add up, parents should get nosy and pry. Changes in your teen's appetite, hours of sleep, and symptoms that seem like an allergy or cold but linger too long, should be explored.

Some parents want to show their children that Mom and Dad are "cool" about drugs. Parents who approve of their own drug use or misuse of medications and alcohol encourage an irresponsible attitude in their kids and set the stage for trouble.

Remember, however, that talk about drugs and other adventurous and dangerous activities are favorite topics for all healthy teenagers. They need this free conversation as a way of exploring these topics easily. Parents and other adults around the teen should not react too impulsively to just talk and save dramatic reactions for a time when the concrete evidence of drug or alcohol use is in.

Volunteering for after-school programs is helpful and allows parents another opportunity to learn what's going on with their kids. Contact your school about its programs. Even an afternoon each week can be a worthwhile contribution.

As a treatment for Attention Deficit Hyperactivity Disorder, Ritalin increases nervous system alertness and thereby increases focus and ability to concentrate. Millions of prescriptions for Ritalin are written each year to treat ADHD. The use of Adderall and Dexedrine is not far behind Ritalin in the totals for ADHD treatment, up 2,000 percent in the last two decades.

Yet a study by Drs. Adrian Angold and Jane Costello found that the majority of children and adolescents who receive these medications do not fully meet the criteria for ADHD—even with the expanded criteria for ADHD approved by the American Psychiatric Association.

Many parents have made medications their first solution to behavior problems. Dr. Lawrence H. Diller, pediatrician and author of Running on Ritalin: A Physician Reflects on Children, Society and Performance in a Pill, concludes: "How we deal with our kids' problems reflects our thinking and a much larger problem in our culture." An editorial in the Journal of the American Medical Association reported that drugs have tripled for children under five, increased 170 percent for five- to 14-year-olds and again up 300 percent for the 15- to 19-year-olds.

Many parents want a solution that requires no more work or attention beyond making sure the troublesome youngster gets his medication. Physicians also hope prescriptions will do the job. The business world hopes to sell caffeine, sugar and additives, regardless of the behavioral effects. Limiting these in your teen's diet may be more effective than medications that have no proven track record with very young persons. For ADHD children who are temporarily so hot-wired they cannot be reached and cannot be taught, Ritalin can be a godsend. And a day in school can go much better for a student who would otherwise wreck a school day for the other students as well.

When absolutely necessary parental time is added, a teenager in need of medication may develop and adjust to life and soon leave the medications behind. However, you will have to defend a distinction between "drugs" and medications in family discussions later on.

Parents need to keep a close eye on the possible sources of problems to be sure medications continue only when and as long as, needed.

The concern about alcohol and drugs also requires strategies focusing on learning what is going on. The effects of experimental drug-taking, for example, are the same symptoms parents see everyday, cold-like symptoms, changes in sleeping and eating patterns, new friends, new attitudes, new demands about money, longer hours at the mall, and hanging out. All are very normal unless they all happen at once.

It's the clustering that should ring an alarm. When the hangout, the mall or corner, suddenly takes much more time, the sniffles become an annoyance to the whole family, demands for new curfew hours increase, and there is money suddenly missing, or suddenly acquired and cannot be explained, it's time to be suspicious.

"Tune in" to your teen's life, habits, and problems. Notice general changes in eating, sleeping, health, and friends.

6. Checklists for Changes Due to Drugs
Checklist Number One: Changes in Habits

1. Does your teenager need more money than usual, or is money missing from the house?
2. Is your teen spending more time in his/her room with the door closed or locked?
3. Have sleeping or eating habits changed or has irritability increased?
4. Has your teenager changed friends or become

secretive about friends?

One mom told me she liked to eat dinner slowly so she and her teenage son could talk. It allowed her to learn about his activities with school and friends. When she saw an unexplained change in his appetite, she asked him about it and found out that he had started stopping off with friends at a fast food restaurant after school. She was put at ease about a possible danger sign.

Watch the Money. The drug business is about money. Where can an unemployed addict get $90 or more a day to support his habit? Recruiting new users is one of the best sources for money. Drug pushers look for teen buyers with extra money, so your teen should carry only the needed amount to school or stores. Listen for information about the amount of money your teen has. Encourage putting money away in savings or shift responsibilities such as buying clothes and personal items to your teen. A bank account for a teen may not seem related to the drug problem, but it is, since a teen with extra money is a tempting target for a frantic user.

Talk With Other Parents. One dad told me he made a point of calling parents of the friends of his daughter, Angie. As a single parent he liked to compare his teen's experiences with what others were going through. He liked to keep up on the latest news but was careful not to tell Angie's secrets because he respected her right to privacy. He knew it was an important part of the trust they shared.

Set an example for your teen to follow in the use of tobacco, alcohol, and drugs. Teens copy you much more than you think. Review your habits for the sake of your teen.

As much as you think your teen will never abuse alcohol or take drugs, you need to know the signs of use. Checklist Number Two contains characteristics that all teens have at one time or another. Abrupt changes in these characteristics should, however, increase your curiosity, and if you're not satisfied, you should be suspicious. This is especially true when these changes occur along with the habits listed in Checklist Number One.

Checklist Number Two: Watch for Changes in Physical Symptoms

1. Lack of concentration; extreme agitation
2. Red eyes, watery eyes, droopy eyelids
3. Runny nose, increased infections and colds
4. Change in sleeping habits—sleeping all day, up all night
5. Slurred or garbled speech, forgetting thoughts or ideas
6. Change in appetite, either increased or decreased; cravings for certain foods
7. Change in activity level; fatigue or hyperactivity
8. Change in appearance, becoming sloppy
9. Lack of coordination, clumsiness, stumbling, sluggishness
10. Shortness of breath, coughing, peculiar odor to breath and clothes

All teens show some variety of these characteristics from time to time so these characteristics do not necessarily indicate drug abuse. The difference that deserves attention is a cluster of abrupt changes.

"John started going with those older kids last

summer and suddenly he didn't care how he looked; he was sloppy, always sniffing, getting up later and later, and he lost interest in everything!"

This mother found drug paraphernalia in her son's room the first time she looked! The cluster of changes in social habits, attitude, and self-care were enough for her to investigate.

7. Depression

The behavior disorder of clinical depression occurs in 4 percent of preschoolers and in about 15 to 20 percent of teenagers. The numbers for teens can be higher than 20 percent because we often brush off their complaints saying they "always talk like that."

The statistics vary partly because the definition of depression varies. Preschoolers don't know the word and, with teenagers, the perception of the word depends on when you talk to them and what they say.

Yet 19 million people in the U.S. complain of depression enough to make it into the clinical medical records. In 2005, 118 million prescriptions for antidepressants were written, twice as many as in 1995, says the Center for Disease Control.

Preschoolers are the fastest growing market for antidepressants. Yet the British Journal of Medicine reported no scientific evidence that antidepressants work for these young children. For children under 18, Britain has banned all but Prozac which is used for complicated emotional problems.

Of course we all get the "blues" and "feel down in the dumps" from time to time. The solution is usually an increase in physical activity—sports or exercise class—or just a change of scene.

For many of us, and especially for teenagers, diet can be a part of the problem. An 11-year-old boy half the weight of his Dad can get far too much sugar from a candy bar or an overdose of fat or caffeine from a portion that would have no effect on his father.

Mental habits can also influence clinical depression. While adults can take encouragement from looking ahead to summer activities or vacations, teenagers are shortsighted. If homework is due tomorrow morning, depression can develop because the prospect of friends coming over tomorrow afternoon is too far in the future as is any upcoming weekend fun.

A teenager's active imagination concerning the magical powers of Harry Potter or the dreams of becoming a soccer star may serve an important antidepressant purpose for a person who has not yet developed the necessary foresight to form realistic goals beyond next week.

In cases where dreams of future success are not enough to pull a grumpy teenager out of depression, a review of activities, diet and mental habits may help parents understand the cause of their teen's depression. Jennifer Conner, psychologist with the Oregon Counseling Organization, lists symptoms of depression such as fatigue, lack of energy, and bad temper. Also, irritability, fear, tension and anxiety are common symptoms as well as a drop in school performance and repeated physical complaints without medical cause (headaches, stomach aches, aching arm or legs).

Of course all of these behaviors occur in all children, but excessive and continuing amounts of these symptoms deserve attention.

Conner suggests seeking immediate professional

advice for serious symptoms, but most depression is usually temporary. Allow your teen space and time. Keep caffeine at absolute zero. Alcohol use by children is never appropriate. Learn more about any medications your teenager is taking. Discourage meal skipping. Regular meals, regular sleep, and regular routines are a crucial part of your teen's ability to cope.

Take time to be a part of your adolescent's physical activity. It will help you as well as them, and it will be an opportunity to listen and understand. Activities such as tennis, swimming, bicycling can last a lifetime. Team sports (soccer, football and baseball) may fade away in the adult years.

Every parent needs to save time for giving attention, communication, and companionship. Consistent supportive attention for a teenager having a low day can make the difference between a habit of depression and a habit of bouncing back.

Communication can be just what the doctor (should have) ordered when a teen needs to tell someone how scary the world sometimes seems. And companionship helps in moments when TV heroes and stars are unattainable and a teenager needs a friend. Love, attention and support from Mom and Dad will help protect a vulnerable teenager from the promises that understanding predators seem to offer. The best thing to spend on your kids is time.

8. Smoking

I haven't seen any plans for tobacco companies to go out of business, so I guess they are counting on somebody's children to fill in for smokers who die off. During the first decade of our new century, nearly 3,000 American teenagers under 18 begin daily smoking each day. In 2014, there was evidence of a growing preference for E-cigarettes among the new teenage smokers. However, this choice still includes nicotine which may lead to addiction to regular cigarettes. If your child delays joining the ranks, there are good consequences.

For example, two teeth. Yes, smokers lose, on the average, two more teeth each decade than nonsmokers. So just delaying smoking from eight until 18 saves two teeth! Of course another 10 teeth are goners in the decades between 18 and 68.

If your children delay smoking until 20, then, in addition to saving two teeth, they are likely to delay turning prematurely gray as well, since smokers are four times more likely to turn gray prematurely. Also delaying smoking will put off balding since men who smoke are twice as likely to be bald or balding as non-smoking men.

In the long term, smokers have thinner, less elastic skin which means more wrinkles than nonsmokers. So children who wait until 25 to start smoking may look ten years younger at age 50 than classmates who started smoking at 15. I guess that's an advantage.

But starting young has other consequences. For example, young smokers have twice the likelihood of colds, flu, and respiratory disorders each year. Young smokers are also much more likely to try marijuana, and teens who have tried marijuana are twice as likely to try other drugs.

If your child delays smoking until 30, other statistics kick in. First, he or she is likely to forget to start smoking at all (more than 80 percent of starters begin in high school, 90 percent before 21).

So when should your child start smoking? The later the better, but never is better than later.

Actually, the percentage of young people starting to smoke hasn't changed much over the decades. But the increasing number of quitters has gone up resulting in an overall decrease in adult smokers in the U.S. from almost 80 percent in 1948 to 44 percent in 1964, to 29 percent in 1987, and 10 to 15 percent today depending on the state.

For all those ex-smokers, the health and longevity benefits start coming right away.

After 20 minutes without smoking, blood pressure decreases, pulse rate drops, body temperature of hands and feet increase.

Eight hours after quitting, carbon monoxide levels in the blood drop to normal and the oxygen level increases to normal. After 24 hours the chance of a heart attack decreases. After two weeks circulation improves and walking is easier.

At one year, the excess risk of heart disease is decreased to half that of a smoker. Five years and stroke risk is down to that of a non-smoker. Ten years and lung cancer risk is down by half. Fifteen years and risk of heart disease and death rate are reduced to almost that of non-smokers.

Mom's and Dad's smoking habits are the biggest factor in children delaying smoking or never starting at all. Over 60 percent of smokers under age 19 are children of parents who smoke (70 percent for girls and 54 percent of boys). Only 35 percent of the smokers under 19 are children of nonsmokers.

So after all the arguing about smoking statistics, what's the best thing a smoking parent can do to steer the kids in the right direction?

Quit.

9. The Battle of the Bulge.

Obesity is an unpleasant word reserved for body fat that's out of control. For children, obesity is reached when total body weight is more than 25 percent fat for boys, 32 percent for girls. Normally, two out of ten children are in this category, but the number can reach eight out of ten children when both of their parents are obese.

In 1970 we Americans fed ourselves on 3,300 calories each day. That was the production from food companies consumed in the USA in those days. Now we are up to 3,800 calories a day according to Marion Nestlé's book, Food Politics: How the Food Industry Influences Nutrition and Health.

The extra 500 daily calories (equivalent to an extra banana split every day) has added 10 pounds to the average weight of a teenager compared with kids of the 90s, says the Pediatricians Research Group of Woodlands, TX. It's not surprising when you consider we tempt ourselves with over 10,000 new food products each year—mostly candy, snacks, soft drinks, baked goods, and ice creams.

Of course exercise enters in. Teenagers who report more than five hours of sedentary TV per day are five times more likely to be overweight than kids watching less than two hours each day. Snacks during TV, say, a small bag of potato chips each day, will add a half pound each week. Not much you might think, but it totals up to a 26-pound weight-gain each year.

The weight problem of our children is bulging

about as fast as their parents' poundage. Back in 1991, when we were each consuming not much more than 3,300 calories per day, only Mississippi, Alabama, and West Virginia had more than 15 percent obese adults. Now more than 20 percent of adults are obese in over half the states.

No doubt the food pushers both at home and in the food business deserve some of the blame for the increases. TV with too many commercials about food and computer time with too much junk food next to the keyboard are bad routines.

Parents can set a slow pace at family meals, even when eating out as much as Americans do. Serving sizes in restaurants are ever larger and parents should keep limits in place even there. The kids could take a doggy bag home, also.

At home, serving water at every meal and having everyone serve their plates, then putting the extra away before sitting down, are healthy habits.

Everything we do requires some effort and inconvenience. All behaviors, even getting out the donuts or hot snack, have an inconvenience. You have to get a plate, find a fork, warm it up, get a drink to go with it.

So keep the healthy food handy and ready—fruit, instead of chips, on the table, ice water instead of soft drinks in the fridge. Let the fat, salt and sugar be the ones that are the most trouble to get from the store and the most troublesome to get out at home. The kids will buy other snacks, but at least at home your diet and their diet will be better.

10. Cars and the Driving Threat

The biggest danger to teenagers, bigger than all the other diseases and accidents of childhood put together, comes when they are almost grown. In the late teenage years, emergency room visits jump from 30 to 60 per million per day and the death rate skyrockets from one per million per day to 10!

The big change is, of course, driving.

A survey by the Liberty Mutual Insurance Company and Students Against Destructive Decisions asked high school students to interview over 1300 teen drivers with accidents or recent near misses. All parents should know the survey results these dedicated students reported after interviewing their fellow drivers.

Over 68 percent of these teens who have had traffic incidents said they were distracted at the crucial moment (47 percent had more than two passengers with them). Sixty-one percent were changing songs on their radio, or CD player. And 36 percent said they were texting when the accident or near miss occurred and the same proportion said they were on their cell phone. Forty-six percent admitted they were speeding.

The number of teenage drivers involved in fatal crashes has decreased almost 55 percent since the highs in years prior to 2005. Nevertheless, 2500 lives are lost every year according to the Centers for Disease Control and Prevention. Graduated licenses that limit night driving and the restriction on the number of passengers for younger teen drivers can take much of the credit for the reduced numbers.

The driving hours of these multi-taskers increases in the summer.

In July and August teens in the Liberty Mutual study averaged 28.6 driving hours per week. In the school year they averaged 16.4 hours. Still only seven percent said summer driving was more dangerous.

Parents insist on using car seats and seat belts with young children, but when the kids turn 16, all parental efforts are overwhelmed and swept aside by the shocking statistics of driving and riding with reckless friends.

Girls are now almost as much at risk as boys. In 1990, 160 of every 1000 under-18 girls wrecked their cars that year and by 2000 the number was 175. The boys are steady at 210 per 1000 per year.

Alcohol abuse plays a large role. The National Center on Addiction and Substance Abuse reports that girls drink just as much as boys—48 percent of girls drink; 52 percent of boys. In 2000, among high school freshmen, girls nudged out the boys for first place in reports of regular drinking—41 percent of girls and 40 percent of boys.

This summer will bring another round of deaths from drunk driving and risky driving. You don't want to wake up in the middle of the night to that terrible phone call, "This is Officer Smith of the State Police, Your daughter (son) has been . . ."

Parents who get that call will pray, in that first heart-stopping moment, that it only involves an arrest or accident and not an injury or death.

The statistics would say Mom and Dad probably gave permission for the driving plan after extracting a few promises—no deviations from the plan, no craziness, and, they might have said, no drinking—but all were likely violated at the fatal moment.

Saying, "Be careful" is not enough. Limitations and restrictions need to be enforced. Better yet, join a parent team that will check on your teen's friends and their evening plans in exchange for your promise to check on yours.

Nothing about safety you have ever done to protect them during all their growing up years is as important as your riding and driving rules.

Mastering use of a car follows the same principles as learning other skills, but your teen places extra value on it. A driving school will help your teen master driving, but you will influence the early practice and a great deal of the long-term habits.

At the first driving session with your teenager he/she can simulate driving. Have him/her sit in the car and pretend starting, braking, and turning the car, to become comfortable with the controls. Talk through a drive around the neighborhood, pretend you accelerate up the hill, pull out around a parked car, and look both ways at the stop sign.

After one or two pretend sessions on the controls and learning permit in hand, have your teen practice driving in an empty parking lot to gain real experience with controls and maneuvering the car. Repeat this several times before moving to the next step. Plan your route each time before starting the car. Most traumatic moments start with a misunderstanding of what was to be done:

> Dad: "Turn here!"
> Teen: "What? Which way?"
> Dad: "Right here!"
> Teen: "Right?"
> Dad: "No, no, left, right here!"
> Teen: "Left, right, make up your mind!"

The next sound you hear in this situation may be

the sound of collapsing metal and plastic. Review plans before taking off. Also review the rules of the road as they apply to parking lots. The most likely minor accident of teens is one in a parking lot where right-of-way is not obvious, and a lot of backing up is required.

Now, before our new driver gets the idea all of this is for free, set up a matching funds program for gasoline, car servicing, driver's license, and insurance fees. And for self-esteem, use your new driver's help with errands and family transportation.

A teen's use of the car is an effective incentive for schoolwork or chores. Work out a plan everyone has a stake in and understands. Earned time can be recorded on the refrigerator door and used as your teen needs it. Instead of taking away earned driving time for poor behavior, use alternatives to punishment.

When Jeff didn't do his big English project, Mom and Dad heard about it and postponed his car use that week. When he completed the report and was up-to-date in his work, he was able to use his accumulated driving time.

Oversee driving practice. When Tom's family

traveled to visit relatives in the next state, he did part of the driving, and when Mom or Dad did local errands, Tom was the chauffeur. Before he had too much time out on his own, Tom had gained valuable experience and he was encouraged for his good driving habits.

Using appropriate speed is especially important to practice. Excessive speed is the most common cause of fatal car accidents. After Barb drove Dad to the mall and back, he praised her. "I felt safe with you driving because you kept to the speed limit. Also, when we stopped at an intersection, I noticed you looked both ways before starting again. So many people run the yellow lights now, a green light doesn't always mean the road will be clear for you."

Mom let Tom know when she felt uneasy riding with him. "Leave more room between yourself and the next car. What if he had to stop suddenly? We'd crash into him!" Over-balance corrections with praise for your teen's good habits to keep a positive feeling.

In spite of your driving model and encouragement of safety, your teen may have poor driving habits. Talk over options to encourage the behavior or limit car use, if that is necessary. Emphasize the desired behavior, but take steps to limit the driving privilege until your teen commits him or herself to the safe driving goal.

Parents' Choice Foundation approves
Teenagers & Parents:
12 Steps to a Better Relationship

"It's a calm read, in an encouraging and guilt-free voice, and it's worth the time, even if everything's going smoothly.

"….the example situations—they're all straightforward and helpful. . . .

"While on the surface, much in his books seems like basic common sense, it's surprising how in the rush of life, common sense can get lost. McIntire recognizes this, without scolding, and reinforces positive behavior—both proactive and reactive—that will ultimately help form healthy kids."

Available as print or e-book on Amazon.com

www.ingramcontent.com/pod-product-compliance
Lightning Source LLC
Chambersburg PA
CBHW050552300426
44112CB00013B/1888